"If you have ever engaged in excessive worry, you will find value in *The Generalized Anxiety Disorder Workbook*. This volume introduces the concepts of intolerance of uncertainty and the search for safety as key aspects of the worry cycle to explain the core processes involved in unwarranted worry. The real jewels of this book, however, are the very many concrete and applicable tools that it provides to readers, to help them both understand their worry and to correct their concerns, if necessary. This workbook is based on solid research as well as the framework of cognitive behavioral therapy (CBT), and is written in an accessible and practical manner by two of the world's leading authorities. I recommend it with no uncertainty."

—**Keith S. Dobson, PhD**, professor of clinical psychology at the University of Calgary, Canada; past president of the Academy of Cognitive Therapy; and past president of the International Association for Cognitive Psychotherapy

"This is a fantastic workbook for several reasons: it is based on a treatment that has strong scientific support from multiple trials; it is brilliantly written, and is highly practical. The downloadable worksheets and exercises, clear examples, and obvious expertise of the authors make this an invaluable resource for people suffering from excessive worry, as well as health professionals."

—**Roz Shafran, PhD**, clinical psychologist and professor of translational psychology at the University College London Institute of Child Health

"*The Generalized Anxiety Disorder Workbook* provides a thorough, engaging, and accessible guide for managing worry. The CBT-based approach is comprehensive, starts from basics, and should have something of value for everyone who struggles with uncontrollable and distressing worry."

—**Graham C. L. Davey, PhD**, professor of psychology at the University of Sussex, United Kingdom

"Everyone who suffers from generalized anxiety disorder (GAD) or has any difficulties with worry should read this book. *The Generalized Anxiety Disorder Workbook* provides an outstanding step-by-step guide to understanding and overcoming worry and anxiety, utilizing scientifically proven techniques and strategies. Robichaud and Dugas are internationally recognized experts who so aptly translate the research findings and practical skills into a workbook that is reader friendly, engaging, and easy to understand. This book should also be required reading for professionals and students interested in the treatment of anxiety."

> —**David J. A. Dozois, PhD**, professor and director of the clinical psychology graduate program in the department of psychology at the University of Western Ontario

"Building on decades of research and their own extensive clinical expertise, Robichaud and Dugas provide easy-to-follow, useful steps that will help people struggling with worry to cope more effectively with those challenges. I highly recommend this book for anyone who feels anxiety is interfering with their lives, and for the therapists who are helping them."

> —**Lizabeth Roemer, PhD**, professor of psychology at the University of Massachusetts Boston, and coauthor of *The Mindful Way Through Anxiety*

THE
GENERALIZED ANXIETY DISORDER WORKBOOK

A Comprehensive CBT Guide for Coping
with Uncertainty, Worry, and Fear

MELISA ROBICHAUD, PhD
MICHEL J. DUGAS, PhD

NEW HARBINGER PUBLICATIONS, INC.

Publisher's Note

NEW HARBINGER PUBLICATIONS is a registered trademark of New Harbinger Publications, Inc.

Distributed in Canada by Raincoast Books

Copyright © 2015 by Melisa Robichaud and Michel J. Dugas
        New Harbinger Publications, Inc.
        5674 Shattuck Avenue
        Oakland, CA 94609
        www.newharbinger.com

Cover design by Amy Shoup
Acquired by Jess O'Brien
Edited by Jasmine Star

Library of Congress Cataloging-in-Publication Data

Names: Robichaud, Melisa. | Dugas, Michel J. (Michel Joseph), 1961-
Title: The generalized anxiety disorder workbook : a comprehensive CBT guide
  for coping with uncertainty, worry, and fear / Melisa Robichaud, PhD, and
  Michel J. Dugas, PhD.
Description: Oakland, CA : New Harbinger Publications, [2015] | Includes
  bibliographical references.
Identifiers: LCCN 2015026340| ISBN 9781626251519 (paperback) | ISBN
  9781626251526 (pdf e-book) | ISBN 9781626251533 (epub)
Subjects: LCSH: Anxiety disorders--Treatment--Handbooks, manuals, etc. |
  Cognitive therapy--Handbooks, manuals, etc. | BISAC: SELF-HELP / Anxieties
  & Phobias. | PSYCHOLOGY / Psychopathology / Anxieties & Phobias.
Classification: LCC RC531 .R59 2015 | DDC 616.85/22--dc23 LC record available at http://lccn.loc.gov/2015026340

Printed in the United States of America

24   23   22

15   14   13   12   11   10   9

Contents

Foreword

It's an honor to contribute this foreword to *The Generalized Anxiety Disorder Workbook*. I treated my first client with generalized anxiety disorder (GAD)—I'll call her "Jacqui"—back in 1989, when I was still a graduate student. Jacqui was not just the first person with GAD I had worked with—she was my first client ever! We used a combination of strategies designed to help Jacqui challenge her anxiety-provoking thoughts and learn to relax, based on several early studies on the treatment of GAD. Despite my lack of experience, Jacqui did well in therapy, experiencing a significant reduction in her worry. This opportunity to work with Jacqui early in my career reinforced for me the value of changing the thoughts and behaviors that maintain problem worry in order to better manage anxiety (both Jacqui's, and that of her brand new therapist-in-training!).

Fast-forward twenty-six years. Effective psychological treatments for GAD are now much better established. They are based on a more refined understanding of the nature of GAD, and are supported by many well-controlled studies, including groundbreaking research by the authors of this book. However, what has remained missing all of these years is a step-by-step self-help workbook describing these proven strategies for overcoming GAD. There are a number of good evidence-based self-help books for dealing with other anxiety-based problems, and for dealing with anxiety in general, but not much for GAD in particular—until now. I've waited more than twenty-five years for this book!

Melisa Robichaud and Michel Dugas have been studying GAD and its treatment for many years, and their treatment is among the best supported by research. A recent controlled study (Dugas et al., 2010) found that after receiving the treatment described in this workbook, 70%

of participants with GAD no longer had GAD at the end of treatment. What's even more amazing is that a year later, 84% of participants no longer had GAD. In other words, people continued to improve in the months after treatment had ended—likely a benefit of continuing to practice the strategies they learned while participating in the study.

I get asked a lot, "Can reading a self-help book really help me overcome my anxiety?" My answer is always the same: "No—no more than reading a book on physical fitness will help you to get physically fit." To experience meaningful, long-term change, it won't be enough to read this workbook. You'll need to practice consistently the strategies described in it. For some readers, it will be possible to benefit from the treatment without the help of a therapist. For others, the support of a therapist will be important for reinforcing the strategies described in the book. Regardless of whether you decide to use this book on its own or in the context of therapy, I highly recommend it for anyone who is struggling with GAD.

Best of luck as you begin your journey toward a life with less anxiety and worry!

Martin M. Antony, PhD, ABPP
Professor, Department of Psychology, Ryerson University
Author, *The Shyness and Social Anxiety Workbook* and *The Anti-Anxiety Workbook*

Introduction

Given that you're reading this book, you're probably someone who struggles with excessive worry and anxiety. You might even have been told by a health professional that you have *generalized anxiety disorder* (GAD), or you might have come to this conclusion on your own, based on things you've read. If so, this book will help you better understand the problem and provide you with concrete strategies for dealing with it.

The approach in this workbook is based on a psychological treatment called *cognitive behavioral therapy* (CBT). A great deal of research has been conducted over the years investigating the effectiveness of CBT for the treatment of anxiety disorders. Overall, the research has shown that CBT is the most effective form of psychological treatment for most if not all anxiety disorders (as well as many other mental health problems). This means the suggestions provided throughout this workbook are evidence based. Stated differently, the suggested strategies are not based on clinical intuition (what we *think* will work); they are based on science.

As you read through this workbook, you might find that some of the points discussed seem obvious or that some of the examples seem overly simplistic. However, this is the result of a deliberate decision on our part. Although most readers will probably have GAD symptoms in common, everyone is nonetheless different, so you are reading this book with your own unique knowledge. And while you might be familiar with many of the concepts discussed, other readers might not. Therefore, we start with the basics so that everyone who uses this workbook will have the same foundation.

In addition, although some of the concepts are relatively straightforward and simple, it may be tricky to practice them in real life. Having a good understanding of the reasoning behind the strategies presented can help ensure that you apply them correctly. Therefore, we have also provided basic, clear, concrete examples, such as fears of flying, getting lost, or going to parties. Your own worries and fears may be more complicated than the examples we provide. However, if you're confident in your understanding of these simple examples, you'll be better able to apply the strategies in this book to your particular worry and anxiety.

How to Use This Workbook

The workbook includes several different strategies, sometimes spread out across multiple chapters. Each strategy is based on a different concept about how to understand and manage worry and GAD. We encourage you to take time to understand the logic behind each new idea. In addition, sometimes we'll ask you to monitor a specific type of thought or behavior prior to learning the strategies associated with a new idea. This monitoring is important, as it will give you a foundation of personal experience that will help you better understand the concepts presented.

For each strategy, we include several exercises, and some of them require a week or two of practice. We strongly encourage you to take the time to master each one before moving on to the next strategy, even if this means you spend several weeks working on just one new approach. Plus, practice will increase your confidence, so feel free to stick with the same idea for as long as you need to. At the same time, if you feel that a concept or approach isn't a good match for you, you need not spend a great deal of time on it. Keep in mind that although some of the ideas in this book might not initially seem relevant to you, they could actually be helpful; so stick with all of the exercises for a while before deciding whether they are helpful or not.

Many of the exercises and worksheets in this book are available for download so that you can use them repeatedly. We've indicated which are available in the text. To download them, visit http://www.newharbinger.com/31519. (See the back of the book for instructions on how to access the files.)

Working on Your Own vs. with a Therapist

You can work your way through this book on your own, or do the work in conjunction with a CBT therapist. However, if you choose to do this work on your own, we recommend that you try to stick to a regular schedule. Specifically, it would be a good idea to set aside a designated time each week to review the exercises you've been working on. At that time, you can decide whether you need to keep working on a particular skill or whether you're ready to move on to the next chapter. When we discuss this review with our clients, we refer to it as having a therapy session with yourself. So pick a relatively regular time and place during your week, perhaps at your favorite coffee shop or at home at a time when you can be alone and focus on yourself for a bit. Plan to give yourself forty-five minutes to an hour. That will allow enough time for you to review the exercises you've been doing, plan new ones, and perhaps read a new chapter or section or reread a previous one.

Why See a CBT Therapist?

There are many benefits to seeing a CBT therapist when you're working on managing your anxiety. First, a therapist can help with motivation and accountability. It can sometimes be a challenge to stick with new things, even if you have the best of intentions. For example, you might have gotten a gym membership in the past, only to go once or twice before eventually giving up. Building any new habit, including using CBT to work on your worries, requires you to stay motivated and follow through from week to week. Seeing a therapist can help with this, since you'll probably have regularly scheduled sessions during which you and your therapist will review and discuss any exercises you worked on over the past week. Because you know your therapist will ask how you did with the exercises, you may be more likely to follow through on them. In addition, if you're having difficulty staying motivated with CBT strategies, you can discuss this with your therapist, who will probably have some ideas about how you can address the issue.

Another advantage of seeing a CBT therapist is that you get the benefit of the therapist's expertise in CBT. If you're struggling with a particular concept or are unsure how to complete an exercise, a therapist can help you troubleshoot the problem and brainstorm solutions. Moreover, because everyone with GAD has unique struggles with worry and anxiety, a CBT therapist can help you tailor the strategies in this book to your specific symptoms. In essence, your therapist can match the different ideas in therapy to your GAD "fingerprint."

When You Should See a Therapist

A good way to approach the CBT strategies described in this workbook is to think of them as the first element in a *stepped care program*. In a stepped care program, you begin by addressing problematic symptoms with a low-intensity treatment. Then, if the problem remains unmanageable, you move to a higher-intensity intervention. This workbook can be considered a low-intensity intervention. It's an ideal tool for people whose GAD symptoms are mild to moderate. In mental health, *mild to moderate symptoms* are those that are severe enough to be distressing to you and interfere with your quality of life, but moderate enough that you can still manage most of your daily activities and muster sufficient concentration to work through the steps in a workbook such as this one.

If instead you feel very overwhelmed by any of the exercises in this workbook, or you're so anxious that you can't even concentrate enough to read some of the material, this is a sign that your GAD symptoms may be too severe for you to do this work by yourself. In this case, a high-intensity intervention might be more appropriate, and that would involve working with a CBT therapist. A therapist will not only help you work through the CBT strategies at your own pace but will also provide support and encouragement throughout the process.

Also, remember that it can be difficult to stay motivated when embarking on a new task. If you find that on several occasions you pick up this book and start on the work only to abandon it halfway through, you might benefit from working with a CBT therapist who can help you stick with it.

All of that said, the ideas and exercises described in this book are, for the most part, relatively simple and straightforward. We believe that the vast majority of readers will truly benefit from implementing the procedures we describe. Having worked with hundreds of clients with GAD over the past two decades, we are very pleased to be in a position to take what we've learned from them and offer it to a wider audience in the form of a workbook. We hope you'll enjoy our book, but most of all we hope it will help you along the road to a life without GAD.

CHAPTER 1

Worry, Anxiety, and GAD

I n order to discuss how to deal with worry, anxiety, and GAD, we need to establish clear definitions of these terms. Most people tend to use the words "worry" and "anxiety" interchangeably, which can make it a challenge to differentiate between them in practical terms. To deal with a problem, you first have to be clear on exactly what the problem is.

Understanding Worry

Worry is a cognitive process: it occurs in the mind. Worry involves mentally anticipating and preparing for potential negative outcomes in the future. For example, let's say you take your car into the shop for a tune-up. You might think, *What if there are major problems with the engine? It could be very expensive, and I might not be able to afford it. I could probably talk to the mechanic about a payment plan. But what if he doesn't accept? I could be without a car for a long time before I could pay for the repairs, and it might be difficult for me to get to work on time without a car.* From this example, you can see that worry involves two components. One is thinking about negative things that could happen and their consequences (in this case, anticipating that your car might need major repairs, and that if you can't afford it, you'll have to figure out alternative transportation to work). The second is problem solving, or mental attempts to deal with these anticipated negative outcomes (thinking about talking to the mechanic about a payment plan).

Worry can therefore be thought of as mentally planning and preparing for the future, and building elaborate scenarios in an effort to predict what could happen and how you might deal with various situations: *What if X happened? Well, then I might do this… But what if Y happened? Then I could do this…* Although there are many different things that people can worry about, all worries tend to share certain characteristics.

Worries typically start as what-if questions. This makes sense, given that when you worry you're trying to mentally plan and prepare by thinking about possible outcomes of potential future situations. For example, if you're planning on taking a trip, you might think, *What if it rains the whole time?* This question then sets off worries: *If it rains, I might not be able to do any of the activities I planned, and I'll have a terrible time. Perhaps I should also think about rainy-day activities. But what if I can't come up with any fun activities for a rainy day?*

Worries are thoughts about the future. Even if you're thinking about a past event, when you're worrying you're concerned about the event's future implications. For example, if you're worrying, about an argument you had with a friend a week ago, you might be thinking, *What if our friendship can never be repaired?* This worry is focused on a possible future impact (the end of the friendship) resulting from a past event (the argument a week before).

Worries are always negative. When you worry about potential future outcomes, you aren't concerned about positive things that could happen (*What if I have a wonderful time on my vacation?*), since they don't require any mental problem solving. Rather, your worries are focused on bad things that could happen. The content of worries therefore tends to be *catastrophic*, meaning you focus on the worst-case scenario even if you logically know that it's very unlikely. For instance, if you're worried about medical test results, you might fear that you have a serious disease, even if the tests are simply part of your annual checkup.

What Triggers Worry?

You might be wondering what triggers worry in the first place, particularly since it's possible to worry about many different types of things. Research has shown that what triggers worries is the experience of unpredictable, novel, or ambiguous events (Inglis 2000; Lee 2001). In other words, you're more likely to worry when you're faced with a situation where the outcome is unclear (unpredictable), where the situation is completely new to you (novel), or where the situation itself isn't very well-defined (ambiguous). In these types of situations, because there's some uncertainty about the outcome, there are many possibilities about what *could* happen, and you don't really know what will occur. Worry is, therefore, an attempt to think about all of these possibilities and mentally develop a plan beforehand. Let's look at an example for each of these uncertainty-inducing situations: unpredictable, novel, and ambiguous.

UNPREDICTABLE SITUATIONS

An example of an *unpredictable situation* might be preparing for a written exam. Since you don't know exactly what questions will be on the exam, the situation is unpredictable: Will the questions be difficult? Will you be anxious when you take the exam? Did you study the right material in order to answer the questions? There's no way to predict exactly what will be on the exam.

In this case, your worries might be *What if I don't study enough for the exam? I could study extra hours every day. But what if I forget something important and it's on the exam? What if I don't understand the questions? I could fail the class!*

Another example of an unpredictable situation is going for a job interview. No matter how much you prepare, you don't know what your potential employer will ask during the interview. As such, you're more likely to worry: *What if she doesn't like me? What if she asks me a question that I don't answer well? I might not get hired.*

NOVEL SITUATIONS

A *novel situation* is any situation that you've never been in before. This can include trying an exercise class you've never taken before, starting a new job, or traveling somewhere you've never been. If, for example, you've never tried sushi and friends invite you to dinner at a sushi restaurant, the novelty of the situation can trigger worries: *What if I don't like sushi? I could end up paying for a meal that I don't eat and then have to get dinner elsewhere. Maybe I could ask the waiter for something simple that someone who's never had sushi might like. But what if I don't like anything in the restaurant? In addition to being hungry, I could be embarrassed in front of my friends.*

Going to college for the first time is another example of situation that's novel and may therefore trigger worries: *What if I get lost when I get there? What if I can't find my class? I could walk in late and embarrass myself. I could get there early to make sure that I find my class and make it on time. But what if the classrooms are so large that I'm overwhelmed by the number of people?*

AMBIGUOUS SITUATIONS

An *ambiguous situation* is one where it's unclear whether something positive, negative, or neutral could happen. For example, if your boss tells you that he wants to meet with you, this is an ambiguous situation because you don't know why he's asked to speak with you. It could be to tell you that you got a raise (positive outcome), to tell you what tasks you need to complete that day (neutral outcome), or to reprimand you for not doing a certain task correctly (negative outcome). Because the situation is ambiguous and you don't know what to expect, you're more likely to worry: *What if he wants to see me because I did something wrong? He could fire me. I could tell him that I'll work harder and not make any more mistakes, but what if he disregards what I say and fires me anyway?*

Another example would be leaving a phone message for a friend and not hearing back from him: Why didn't he contact you? Perhaps he didn't receive the message, or maybe he called you back and you somehow didn't get the message. However, it's also possible that he doesn't want to speak to you, is angry with you for some reason, is overwhelmed with some sort of life problem, or is simply very busy. Because you don't know why your friend didn't return your call, this is an ambiguous situation that's likely to lead to worry: *What if he didn't get my message? Perhaps I can phone him again and leave another message. But what if he hasn't contacted me because he's very busy right now, and he gets upset that I keep calling? What if he's angry with me and yells at me when I call?*

When Is Worry a Problem?

It's important to remember that everyone worries on occasion, and this is absolutely normal. For instance, we all tend to worry more during times of stress or major life changes. You might find that you're more likely to worry when you have an increase in work responsibilities, during exams, when someone in your family is ill, or when there's a significant event in your life, such as moving to a new home or getting married. In addition, most people sometimes worry when faced with unpredictable, novel, or ambiguous situations. The fact that you worry isn't evidence that there's a problem.

So when does worry become a problem? In the field of mental health, we consider worry to be problematic when it is present most every day, is excessive given the situation, is difficult to control, and interferes with a person's daily life or leads to significant distress. If, for example, you worry about an upcoming exam so much that you can't concentrate on studying, or you're so worried about a job interview that you cancel the interview altogether, it's likely that you have problematic worry. A reduction in quality of life can also signal a problem with worry. You might find that it's hard to enjoy the time you spend with loved ones because you're so preoccupied with worries, or you might find yourself avoiding pleasant activities because you don't want to worry about them beforehand. For example, some people report being so worried about the health and well-being of their children that even when they're playing with their kids, they're focused on their worries rather than on having fun.

EXERCISE 1.1: Assessing Whether Your Worry Is Problematic

As with most symptoms in mental health, problematic worry is a matter of degree. It isn't just the act or presence of worry that indicates a problem, but rather the frequency, severity, excessiveness, and uncontrollability of worry. The following quiz will help you determine whether your worries are problematic. Check off each statement that generally reflects your experience with worry.

_____ I worry most days.

_____ I worry even when everything is okay. (An example would be worrying about your health even when there's nothing wrong.)

_____ I worry too much about small problems. (An example would be worrying a lot about being on time for appointments.)

_____ My worry is excessive. In my opinion, I worry more than I should.

_____ Other people tell me that I worry too much

_____ My worry is hard to control. Once I start worrying, it's hard to stop, even if I try.

If you agreed with at least three of the statements, worry might be a problem for you.

Understanding Anxiety

Whereas worries take place in the mind, anxiety occurs in the body. Anxiety is the general name for a varied number of physical sensations that people experience when they're in danger or feel threatened in some way. Anxiety sensations can include a racing heart, changes in breathing, stomach problems (ranging from butterflies in the stomach to nausea or diarrhea), sweating, trembling or shaking, hot flushes or cold chills, general feelings of restlessness or jumpiness, and dizziness or light-headedness. Anxiety is part of a larger system in the body designed to respond to threats and danger. This threat detection system is sometimes called the *fight-or-flight response*, and it does exactly what the name suggests: it prepares you to either fight a threat, or to run away or flee from it. All of the physical sensations associated with anxiety are actually the body's way of physically preparing you to act in case of danger.

The Problem with Anxiety

Because anxiety is part of the body's threat detection system, it's one of the most important survival mechanisms you have. It's present in some form in all creatures on Earth. It functions to get you out of danger as quickly as possible; for example, it will help you run as fast as you can if you're being chased by a bear. Unfortunately, there are two major problems with the anxiety system.

The first problem with anxiety is that it's triggered anytime you *think* you're in danger, even though you may not actually *be* in danger. Have you ever heard a noise in your home and thought someone was breaking in, only to discover it was something else, like the wind or a pet knocking something over? In the moment when you thought someone was breaking in, you probably felt a jolt of anxiety as your body reacted to the fact that you thought you were in danger. Because the threat detection system reacts to thoughts, it can misfire. In other words, it's possible to feel anxious when there's no real danger.

ANXIETY: YOUR BODY'S SMOKE DETECTOR

A good way to think of anxiety is as the body's smoke detector. Smoke detectors can alert you when there's a fire in your house, allowing you to get out as quickly as possible.

However, smoke detectors don't go off only when there's a fire; they go off anytime there's smoke. You've probably experienced a false alarm in your home, perhaps if you burned toast in your kitchen. The problem is that smoke detectors make the same noise whether there's a real fire or just a false alarm.

Anxiety works the same way: You can feel anxious when you're in danger, but you can also feel anxious when you think you're in danger but actually aren't. So anxiety really only tells you that you *might* be in danger. As with smoke detectors, it's a good idea to investigate further to see whether there's a real danger or it's just a false alarm.

ANXIETY IN THE MODERN WORLD

The second problem with anxiety is that it's really only an ideal mechanism for coping with physical danger. If you're being attacked and need to fight or run away, the fight-or-flight response does a great job of preparing your body to do so. However, as human beings in the modern world, our day-to-day threats usually aren't physical. Instead, we are most concerned about social threats and dangers that we anticipate in our minds.

For example, you might worry about being late for work and potentially making your boss angry, or you might be worried about what you'll talk about when meeting new people at a party. Both of these situations can cause anxiety, but neither is actually a physical threat; you aren't concerned that your boss will be so angry or new people so unfriendly that they'll physically harm you. Yet you still feel anxiety. This is because humans have only one threat detection system in the body, and it doesn't differentiate between physical and social threats.

Although anxiety is excellent for propelling you into action when physical danger is present, it's less than ideal when the threat is social or triggered by worries. Unfortunately, because the fight-or-flight response is activated whenever you feel threatened, your first impulse will probably be to flee and avoid the threat, whatever its nature. When it comes to daily life worries, this is often an unhelpful strategy that can actually make your worries worse over time.

Anxiety Disorders: When Anxiety Becomes a Problem

Anxiety is similar to worry in that simply being anxious doesn't mean you have a problem. As discussed, the physical sensations of anxiety are necessary for protection from danger. In addition, it's also normal to experience anxiety on occasion in unpredictable, novel, or ambiguous situations. For example, you were probably quite anxious the first time you drove a car because you had never driven before. This happens to everyone. Although it can be a nuisance to feel anxiety in situations that aren't physically dangerous, it only becomes problematic when you experience this frequently and it impairs you in your daily life. For example, if you drop out of a class due to anxiety about having to give a presentation, then anxiety is interfering in your life. A diagnosis of an anxiety disorder may sometimes be warranted in such cases.

There are several different types of anxiety disorders, and they are largely distinguished by what's causing the anxiety. For example, if fear of germs leaves you severely anxious after touching a doorknob or shaking someone's hand, you might have *obsessive-compulsive disorder*. If you get extremely anxious whenever you need to get an injection at the doctor's office or perhaps avoid necessary injections altogether, you might have a *specific phobia*—in this example, fear of needles or injections. In both cases, the experience of anxiety is the same: anxiety feels like anxiety no matter what the cause is. As such, it's the *trigger* for the anxiety, or the *theme of the threat*, that determines which anxiety disorder is diagnosed.

Anxiety Disorders: A Matter of Degree

It's important to understand that mental health symptoms aren't like a light switch, being either on or off. Such symptoms are seldom completely present or completely absent. Rather, they are present to different degrees in all individuals. Therefore, a symptom like worry falls on a continuum ranging from little or no worry to severe or disabling worry, as shown in figure 1.1, and everyone can be placed somewhere on that line. Receiving a diagnosis of GAD implies that a person's worry is at the high end of the continuum, which in turn implies that the goal of treatment is to help that person shift his or her worry and anxiety into the moderate or low range of the continuum.

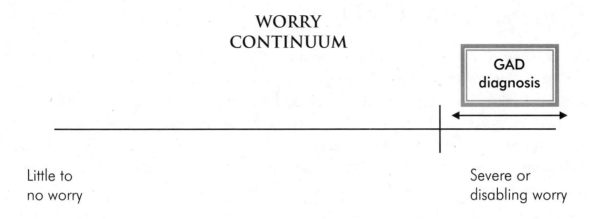

FIGURE 1.1. The worry continuum.

As for who specifically gets an anxiety disorder diagnosis, in mental health we draw a line on the continuum and determine that those past the line probably warrant a diagnosis. In our clinical practice, we view this line as fuzzy because it only represents a clinical threshold: past a certain point of severity, if you find that your symptoms cause you significant distress and interfere with your life, you receive an anxiety disorder diagnosis. The benefit of a diagnosis is that it gives both the person diagnosed and mental health professionals a common language that can explain what the person is struggling with and guide treatment. However, there's no real difference between people on either side of the line; diagnosis is a *matter of degree*. All people with GAD are not the same, just as all people without GAD are not the same. The goal of this workbook is therefore not to "cure" you, but to help you bring your worries and anxiety into a more appropriate and functional range so that you worry less, are less anxious, and aren't distressed and impaired by these symptoms in your daily life.

Understanding GAD

Although we've discussed anxiety disorders in general, the focus of this workbook is on one particular anxiety disorder, generalized anxiety disorder, or GAD. Contrary to its name, the primary symptom of GAD isn't anxiety, but rather excessive and uncontrollable worry about day-to-day events. In GAD, worry is chronic, meaning excessive worry has been present for at least six months and isn't solely due to a stressor in the person's life. There are six physical symptoms that people with GAD can experience, although only three must be present to meet the criteria for diagnosis:

- Feeling restless, keyed up, or on edge

- Being easily fatigued

- Difficulty concentrating or mind going blank

- Irritability

- Muscle tension

- Sleep disturbances

These physical symptoms are experienced chronically, meaning that they are present more days than not for at least six months. Finally, worry and anxiety symptoms need to cause significant distress and impairment in a person's daily life in order to meet the criteria for a GAD diagnosis (American Psychiatric Association 2013).

EXERCISE 1.2: Assessing Your GAD Symptoms

If you think you might have GAD, but aren't sure, the following questionnaire will shed some light on this. (It is reprinted, with permission, from Dugas et al. 2001.) We encourage you to fill out the questionnaire even if you've already been given a diagnosis of GAD. This will give you a baseline for the severity of your symptoms. Later in the book, after you've tried some of the strategies we provide, we'll ask you to fill out the questionnaire again so you can assess your progress.

WORRY AND ANXIETY QUESTIONNAIRE

1. What subjects do you worry about most often?

    a. _____

    b. _____

    c. _____

    d. _____

    e. _____

    f. _____

    For the following items, please circle the corresponding number (0 to 8).

2. Do your worries seem excessive or exaggerated?

    Not at all excessive   Moderately excessive   Totally excessive
    0 .... 1 .... 2 .... 3 .... 4 .... 5 .... 6 .... 7 8

3. Over the past six months, how many days have you been bothered by excessive worry?

    Never   One day out of two   Every day
    0 .... 1 .... 2 .... 3 .... 4 .... 5 .... 6 .... 7 8

4. Do you have difficulty controlling your worries? For example, when you start worrying about something, do you have difficulty stopping?

    No difficulty   Moderate difficulty   Extreme difficulty
    0 .... 1 .... 2 .... 3 .... 4 .... 5 .... 6 .... 7 8

5. Over the past six months, to what extent have you been disturbed by the following symptoms when you were worried or anxious? Rate each symptom by circling a number (0–8).

a. Restlessness or feeling keyed up or on edge

Not at all	Moderately	Very severely

0 .... 1 .... 2 .... 3 .... 4 .... 5 .... 6 .... 7 8

b. Being easily fatigued

Not at all	Moderately	Very severely

0 .... 1 .... 2 .... 3 .... 4 .... 5 .... 6 .... 7 8

c. Difficulty concentrating or mind going blank

Not at all	Moderately	Very severely

0 .... 1 .... 2 .... 3 .... 4 .... 5 .... 6 .... 7 8

d. Irritability

Not at all	Moderately	Very severely

0 .... 1 .... 2 .... 3 .... 4 .... 5 .... 6 .... 7 8

e. Muscle tension

Not at all   Moderately   Very severely

0 .... 1 .... 2 .... 3 .... 4 .... 5 .... 6 .... 7 8

f. Sleep disturbance (difficulty falling or staying asleep or restless unsatisfying sleep)

Not at all   Moderately   Very severely

0 .... 1 .... 2 .... 3 .... 4 .... 5 .... 6 .... 7 8

6. To what extent does worry or anxiety interfere with your life? For example, your work, social activities, family life, and so on?

Not at all   Moderately   Very severely

0 .... 1 .... 2 .... 3 .... 4 .... 5 .... 6 .... 7 8

To meet criteria for GAD, you must endorse the following criteria (check all that apply):

☐ At least two worry topics on item 1

☐ A score of 4 or higher on items 2, 3, 4, and 6

☐ A score of 4 or higher on at least three of the symptoms on item 5

If you checked all three boxes, you meet the criteria required for a diagnosis of GAD.

Taking a Closer Look at GAD Symptoms

You may wonder what GAD looks like in practical terms. Let's consider some of the symptoms one by one, in greater depth.

WORRY ABOUT DAY-TO-DAY EVENTS

People with GAD worry about the same types of things that everybody else does: family, work or school, finances, their health and the health of loved ones, relationships with friends or colleagues, and minor matters, such as punctuality or making small decisions. The difference is that they worry more than people without GAD. If you have GAD, you've probably found that your worries are always in the background. Some days you might worry more and some days you might worry less, but you probably won't have a significant period of time where you aren't worrying about something. You might also notice that what you worry about changes from day to day depending on the situations you're encountering in your life. In our clinical practice, we talk about worry being like music that's constantly playing: the songs may change from hour to hour or day to day, and the volume may be higher or lower, but you can always hear it in the background.

EXCESSIVE AND UNCONTROLLABLE WORRY

It can be challenging to identify when worry is excessive or uncontrollable because these are very subjective terms. However, as a general rule, worries in GAD are deemed excessive if you worry more than is appropriate to the situation, if you worry even when nothing is wrong, or if others have told you that you worry too much. You might have noticed, based on that description, that excessive worry is more than just worrying a lot. For example, if you've just lost your job and don't have enough money to pay your bills, it wouldn't be surprising if you were worried about your finances; that would be appropriate to the situation. But if you haven't lost your job or experienced other financial setbacks and you're worrying all the time about your finances, your worry might be excessive.

In terms of worry being uncontrollable, this refers to how difficult it is for you to stop worrying once you start. When worry isn't problematic, you can often choose to put your worries aside and either not think about them at all or think about them at some other time. If you have GAD, worries are like a freight train: once they get started, it's difficult to put on the brakes. So even if you want to shelve your worries or not think about them at all, you'll probably find that extremely difficult to do, if not impossible. In fact, you might engage in a number of time-consuming and effortful behaviors to try to turn off your worries, such as keeping busy, calling a friend, going for a walk, or any other action that helps keep you distracted from your thoughts. However, if you're like many of the people with GAD whom we've seen, you've probably found that these strategies work only in the short term, if at all.

CHRONIC WORRY

For people with GAD, worry isn't something they do from time to time. Rather, it's a constant companion in their lives. Although this isn't the case for everyone, if you have GAD, you've probably realized that you've been a worrier all your life. You also might have noticed that the severity of your worries has increased over the years. This is common and usually happens because responsibilities tend to increase as life goes on, creating new topics to worry about. Many of our clients report that each of the positive milestones in their lives—becoming an adult, going to college, entering the workforce, getting married, and starting a family—brought an increase in their worries. Over time, this escalation in the frequency and severity of worry can become increasingly unmanageable.

SLEEP PROBLEMS AND FATIGUE

Many people with GAD report that they have a difficult time either falling asleep or staying asleep. If you have a hard time falling asleep, you might find that the minute you put your head to the pillow, worries start spinning in your head. This is because when you're at rest, your mind is free to start worrying. You might find that you actually worry less during the day when you're busy, since you're distracted by other things. However, your worries aren't gone; they're just pushed to the back of your mind, only to spring forward again when you're trying to relax and are no longer distracted.

Some people find that their problem is staying asleep. They may wake up several times a night, sometimes awoken by their worries. Even when you sleep, your mind is still working, and whatever you worried about that day can carry over into the night.

Because it's exhausting to worry excessively and because it's common for people with GAD to have sleep problems, it isn't surprising that you might be easily fatigued. In many ways, having GAD is like walking around with a sack of potatoes on your back; in addition to all the normal stresses of life, you're carrying around extra worries most every day, usually for months or years on end, and this can lead to a sense of being easily fatigued and drained.

DIFFICULTIES WITH CONCENTRATION

When you're anxious, your mind automatically starts to selectively shift its attention toward threats. For example, if you're walking down a dark street at night and aren't feeling safe, you'll immediately be more aware of potential signs of danger, such as alleyways or dark corridors where someone could be lurking. At the same time, your attention is diverted away from things that aren't directly threatening, so you may not notice any of the shops you pass. It's a bit like looking at the world through a microscope: you can see small, specific parts very clearly, but because the focus is so small, you miss the big picture entirely. So how does this apply to GAD? Because you're so focused on your worries, and because your attention zeros in on threats when you're anxious, it can be very challenging to concentrate on day-to-day tasks.

FEELING RESTLESS, KEYED UP, OR ON EDGE

If you are chronically worried, then you probably also feel anxious throughout the day. Given that anxiety reflects activation of the fight-or-flight response, your body is therefore physically preparing to face a threat. In practical terms, this means you'll probably feel jumpy, restless, and on edge as your body readies itself to either face danger or flee from it.

Surprisingly, these feelings of restlessness or agitation often aren't noticed by others, which makes GAD a deceptively functional problem, where you appear as if you're doing well while on the inside you feel anxious and on edge. In essence, having GAD is a bit like being a duck swimming on a lake: although ducks might look calm as they glide along the surface of the lake, their webbed feet are working furiously underwater.

IRRITABILITY

You might find that you're easily irritated and often have a tendency to snap at people, sometimes over insignificant things. This is a by-product of being anxious and worried most every day. When you worry, your mind is focused on potential threats and how you might avert them. Then, if there's a small change in plans or if someone talks to you about something that's unrelated to whatever you're worried about, you're more likely to be annoyed and impatient. A good way to think about this is to use a physical threat as an example. If you were walking in the woods and thought you saw a bear in the distance, you'd become anxious and your thoughts would focus on figuring out how to deal with the situation. If at that moment someone came up to ask you what you'd like to have for dinner that night, you'd probably snap at the person; the question would feel like a distraction at that time. This same logic applies to day-to-day life when you're worried.

Many people we see in our practice are concerned that their bouts of irritability are a sign that they're generally negative, pessimistic, or unfriendly. This isn't the case. GAD isn't associated with pessimism. While the content of worry is always negative in nature, this doesn't mean you're a negative person. Rather, you think negative thoughts when you're anxious. Again, although this is adaptive when you're physically threatened, it isn't helpful in daily life.

MUSCLE TENSION

People with GAD often report that they have muscle tension, usually in their neck and shoulders or in their jaw. This is the result of being chronically anxious: when you're anxious, you're more likely to tense your muscles, which in this case translates into raising your shoulders or tightening your jaw muscles. If you've been doing this throughout the day for several months, it wouldn't be surprising if you had physical discomfort due to muscle tension.

Tracking Your Worries

Because worries are the main feature of GAD, it's important to understand your particular pattern of worry. What sorts of things do you worry about? Do certain worries come up more than others? What typically triggers your worries? How anxious do your worries make you? In order to answer these questions, you need to get a good idea of what you worry about on a day-to-day basis. *Worry monitoring* is an excellent tool for accomplishing this, as it will allow you to get a "slice of life" with respect to your worries and begin to identify any patterns to your worry that you may not have noticed.

EXERCISE 1.3: Keeping a Worry Monitoring Log

Worry monitoring involves tracking your worries several times a day for at least one week. It doesn't involve writing down every worry you have; instead, you record just three worries per day. The purpose is to get a snapshot of your worry patterns, not a detailed description of everything you worry about.

We've provided a Worry Monitoring Log you can use for this purpose. (A downloadable version is available at http://www.newharbinger.com/31519.) Alternatively, you can record the same information in a small notebook that you can carry with you or with an electronic device. Use whichever method is easiest for you.

Here's an example of one day's worth of entries in a Worry Monitoring Log.

SAMPLE WORRY MONITORING LOG

Date and time	Situation or trigger	Worry (what if?)	Anxiety (0 to 10)
Sunday 9:30 a.m.	Planning a to-do list for the day	What if I don't get everything done today? That would be terrible.	6
Sunday 3 p.m.	At home; the phone rings	What if it's bad news? I wouldn't be able to handle it.	5
Sunday 10 p.m.	Thinking about an upcoming exam	What if I didn't study enough for the exam? I could fail the class.	8

There are four columns in the form:

1. **Date and time:** In this column, record when the worry occurred.

2. **Situation or trigger:** In this column, record what was going on when you started to worry.

3. **Worry (what if?):** In this column, briefly describe your worry. Notice that in the example, only a couple of thoughts are recorded for each worry, not the entire thought process. Again, this exercise is meant to help you begin to see your worry patterns; it isn't meant to be a time-consuming or difficult task. Just write down your first few thoughts to provide a snapshot of some of your daily worries.

4. **Anxiety (0 to 10):** In this final column, record how anxious you became because of your worry. A rating of 0 means you weren't anxious at all, a rating of 5 reflects moderate anxiety, and a rating of 10 means you were extremely anxious.

Tips for Filling Out a Worry Monitoring Log

Tip 1: Only complete the log three times a day. You might be concerned that you won't get an accurate picture of your worries if you don't fill it out more often, but this isn't necessary. Remember, you're just obtaining a slice of life. The goal isn't to write down every one of your worries; it's just to get a general idea of the kinds of worries you have from day to day.

Tip 2: Use your anxiety as a cue. You might be surprised to know that it can sometimes be difficult to even catch yourself worrying long enough to then write down the worry. If you have GAD, worrying is such a constant part of your life that you might not always be aware that you're doing it. However, you are likely to notice when you start feeling anxious. Therefore, it can be helpful to use the feeling of anxiety as a cue to observe your worries and identify the situation that might have triggered them. A good habit to get into is to notice whenever you feel anxious and then ask yourself, "What am I worrying about *right now?*"

Tip 3: Write down your worries as soon as you can. One of the most important parts of completing your Worry Monitoring Log is to do so as soon as reasonably possible. Obviously, you can't fill it out while driving or when in the middle of a conversation. However, what you write down will most accurately reflect your actual worry when the thought is fresh in your mind. If you wait a day or two, you might forget how anxious you were, what originally triggered the worry, or even the content of the worry itself. Therefore, if you forget to write down your worries one day, don't record items from that day on the next day. It's better to let that day go and accurately record your current worries than to rely on your memory of what you think you worried about.

WORRY MONITORING LOG

Date and time	Situation or trigger	Worry (what if?)	Anxiety (0 to 10)

Recognizing Worry Types

You already know that you can worry about a number of different topics—your health, your family, your job, your finances, and the list goes on. But for the purposes of your work with this book, it's also extremely helpful to divide worries into two categories: worries about current problems and worries about hypothetical situations. Although this distinction will become more important later in the book, when we introduce different strategies for each of these worry types, it's good to understand the difference between the two right from the start.

Worries About Current Problems

Worries about current problems involve concerns about problematic situations you're dealing with in the here and now. Here are a couple of examples:

- *I put in fewer hours at work these past two weeks. What if I can't pay all my bills at the end of the month?*

- *I'm having a hard time finishing an assignment for class. What if I don't get it done on time?*

In these situations, you're struggling with a real problem and you have some degree of control over the situation, so there are probably things you can do to resolve the problem. For example, if your worries involve not paying bills on time, potential solutions include borrowing money, asking for an advance at work, or deferring a regular monthly payment.

Worries About Hypothetical Situations

In contrast to worries about current problems, worries about hypothetical situations involve things that haven't happened yet—and may never happen. They tend to involve situations in the more distant future that you have little to no control over. Here are two examples:

- *I'm taking a flight next month. What if the plane crashes?*

- *What if someone in my family gets sick and I can't cope?*

In contrast to current problems, there's little you can do to deal with these situations because they simply do not yet exist. As such, there's nothing in the situation to apply problem solving to. You can't predict whether your plane will crash or how you'll cope with the loss of a loved one, and any preparation won't be useful if the situation never materializes.

EXERCISE 1.4: Identifying Your Worry Types

Not surprisingly, strategies that can be helpful for managing worries about real problems probably won't be very helpful for worries about hypothetical situations. Therefore, later in this book we'll discuss each worry type and how to cope with it in a separate chapter. For this reason, it's a good idea to go ahead and get some practice with discriminating between these two worry types. To help with this, write down which worry type (about a current problem or a hypothetical situation) these examples might fall under.

1. *My sister is late coming home. What if she got into a car accident?*

   Current problem or hypothetical situation? _____

2. *I forgot to pick up some groceries at the store, and I'm having people over for dinner tonight. If I go to the store now to pick up the missing items, I won't have much time to cook. What if I don't have dinner prepared by the time my guests arrive?*

   Current problem or hypothetical situation? _____

3. *My doctor told me that I should try to exercise regularly. What if I can't find the time to exercise like my doctor suggested?*

   Current problem or hypothetical situation? _____

You might have found this exercise a bit of a challenge. It isn't always easy to distinguish between worry types. A helpful strategy can be to think about whether the situation is a confirmed problem that has already taken place or is only a potential problem that hasn't happened yet and may not ever happen. You can also think about how much control you actually have in the situation. In other words, is there something that you can realistically do to deal with the situation? If there isn't, the worry is probably about a hypothetical situation. Using this logic, the preceding worries could be classified as follows.

1. *My sister is late coming home. What if she got into a car accident?*

   This looks like a worry about a hypothetical situation. You don't know whether your sister got into a car accident, and there's nothing that you can do to change that if it happened. As such, this is a potential problem, not a confirmed problem. Worries about hypothetical situations reflect potential problems that may not happen.

2. *I forgot to pick up some groceries at the store, and I'm having people over for dinner tonight. If I go to the store now to pick up the missing items, I won't have much time to cook. What if I don't have dinner prepared by the time my guests arrive?*

   This looks like a worry about a current problem. You did in fact forget to pick up all the items from the grocery store that you needed to make dinner, so this is a confirmed problem. Moreover, you have some control over what you serve for dinner, whether or not you can go to the grocery store, whether to send someone else, or whether to postpone the dinner.

3. *My doctor told me that I should try to exercise regularly. What if I can't find the time to exercise like my doctor suggested?*

   This looks like a worry about a current problem. This one is a little tricky, since it isn't clear whether you actually don't have enough time to exercise regularly or are just worried that you might not have time to exercise. However, since the doctor has recommended that you exercise and you probably aren't doing so already, this seems to be a confirmed problem. Moreover, you have direct control over this situation. You have control over your own schedule, and therefore you have control over when you might exercise and what type of exercise you could do. All of this is further evidence for the fact that this is a current problem.

EXERCISE 1.5: Looking at Your Worry Types

After you've filled out your Worry Monitoring Log for one week, take a few moments to review each worry and try to determine whether it's a worry about a current problem or a hypothetical situation. You might want to write down CP (current problem) or HS (hypothetical situation) next to each worry you recorded. In addition to giving you some practice in differentiating between these two worry types, it will also tell you something about your worry patterns. Perhaps you worry more about current problems or more about hypothetical situations, or perhaps you experience both worry types relatively equally.

One final note: Even if you find it difficult, try to pick a type for each one of your worries. You might second-guess yourself or want to write down that a worry is a bit of both, but as you'll soon see, making a choice, even when you aren't completely sure, is a good thing to practice.

CHAPTER 2

CBT for GAD

Cognitive behavioral therapy, or CBT, is the psychological treatment of choice for GAD. If you're unfamiliar with CBT, it's important to have a good understanding of what it is, what it involves, and the time and commitment required of you for success. Much of CBT is based on logical ideas, and if these ideas don't make sense to you, CBT is unlikely to be maximally helpful. This chapter is therefore devoted to explaining some basic principles of CBT that will help you better understand the strategies you'll apply to your chronic worry and anxiety as you work with this book.

The Basics of CBT

CBT is based on the simple concept that in most every situation you experience in your life, you have certain thoughts, feelings, and behaviors, and that these three parts of you interact and influence each other. Because of this relationship, when you can recognize and identify the thoughts and behaviors that lead to your feelings of distress, such as fear and anxiety, you can learn to change your ways of thinking and behaving to reduce your negative feelings. A good way to understand this is with the ABC triangle, in which ABC stands for *affect* (feelings, or emotions), *behavior* (actions), and *cognition* (thoughts).

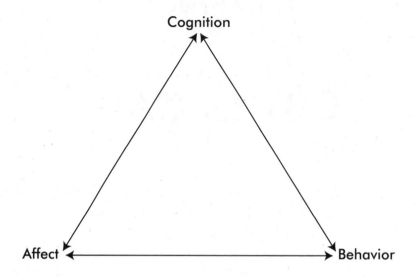

FIGURE 2.1.

To illustrate the interaction between thoughts, feelings, and behaviors, consider the following situation: You're walking down the street, and you see your cousin in the distance. If you happen to like your cousin, you might think, *Hey, that's my cousin! What a great coincidence to see her here.* This thought will probably make you feel happy, and you might wave to her and call out her name.

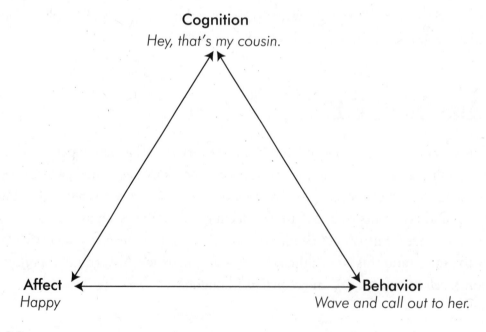

FIGURE 2.2.

However, as you keep walking down the street and get closer to the person you're waving to, you suddenly realize that the person is not in fact your cousin. Then you might think, *That's not my cousin! I've just been waving to a complete stranger.* This thought might make you feel embarrassed, and you'd probably stop waving and maybe apologize or tell the person you thought she was someone else.

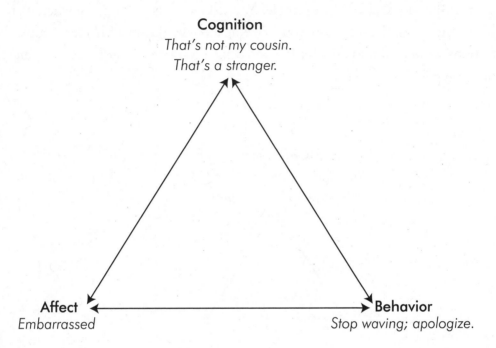

FIGURE 2.3.

One thing to notice about this example is that the situation didn't change. You were walking down the street and you saw someone in the distance. What changed was what you thought and, as a consequence, what you did and how you felt.

Characteristics of the ABC Triangle

There are several characteristics of the relationship between thoughts, feelings, and behaviors that will come into play when you start applying the logic of the ABC triangle to your particular worry and anxiety symptoms, so it's best to understand them right from the start.

A RECIPROCAL RELATIONSHIP

In the example of walking down the street and thinking that you recognize someone you know, that thought had an effect on your emotions and behaviors. However, the relationship between thoughts, feelings, and behaviors is reciprocal, meaning that influence runs in both directions, so each point of the triangle can influence the other two. To illustrate this, let's look at a new example. You decide to go to a party where you won't really know anyone, and once there, you strike up a conversation with a few people. If your conversations go well, you might think, *I'm having a good time, and I'm glad I came to this party*, and you might feel happy.

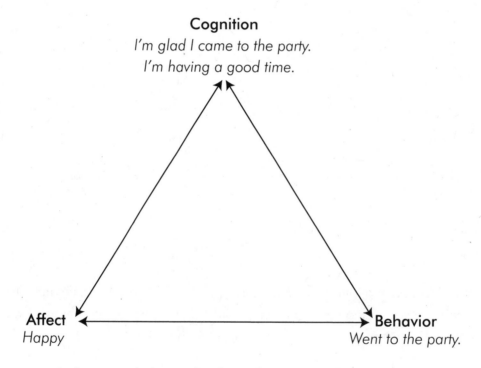

FIGURE 2.4.   A change in behavior leads to changes in affect and cognition.

If, on the other hand, you felt very anxious before going to the party, this feeling could then influence your thoughts and behaviors. You might decide not to go to the party, and perhaps you'd think, *I probably wouldn't have a good time if I went*.

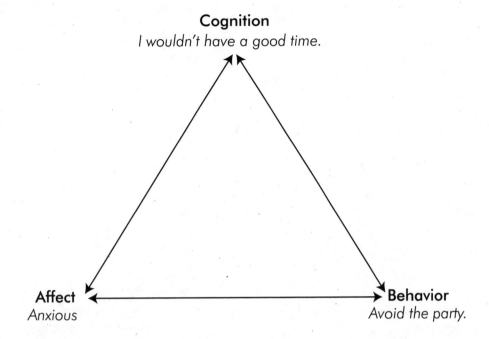

Cognition
I wouldn't have a good time.

Affect
Anxious

Behavior
Avoid the party.

FIGURE 2.5. A change in affect leads to changes in behavior and cognition.

VICIOUS CYCLE

Another property of the relationship between thoughts, feelings, and behaviors is that the cycle can repeat and amplify. Let's say you had an argument with a friend. The next day your phone rings, and you see that your friend is calling. You might think, *She's probably calling to yell at me*, which would probably make you anxious. As a result, you may avoid picking up the phone. When you avoid the phone call, you'll feel less anxious in the moment, but then you might think, *If she knows I was avoiding her phone call, she'll probably be really upset with me*, which might make you even more anxious. You might even call another friend to ask for advice.

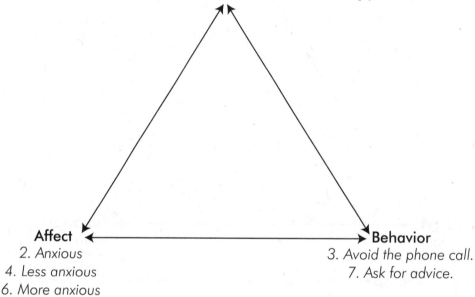

Cognition
1. She's calling to yell at me.
5. She knows I'm avoiding her, and she'll be angry.

Affect
2. Anxious
4. Less anxious
6. More anxious

Behavior
3. Avoid the phone call.
7. Ask for advice.

FIGURE 2.6.

This back-and-forth interaction between thoughts, feelings, and behaviors can be described as a *vicious cycle*, since each of the three points of the triangle has an increasingly negative impact on the other two. In all likelihood, if your friend phones again your anxiety will be higher than the first time she called, making the situation even more difficult.

This vicious cycle may look discouraging, given that your thoughts, feelings, and behaviors can get caught in a downward spiral and become increasingly negative. However, it's actually good news, since the cycle can work in a positive direction as well. For example, if instead of avoiding your friend's call you decided to answer the phone, you'd probably feel more anxious at first. However, if she was calling to resolve the argument and apologize for the misunderstanding, you might feel relieved and tell yourself, *I was wrong. She had no intention of yelling at me.* You might then apologize too, perhaps telling yourself, *Next time I won't jump to conclusions so quickly.* As a result, if you were to experience another situation where you felt anxious when someone phoned you, you might find it easier to pick up the phone and resolve the issue.

THE MEANING OF THE SITUATION

When you were reading the preceding example, you might have said to yourself, *I would have thought my friend was calling to make up after the fight, not to yell at me*. In that case, you wouldn't have seen the phone call as an anxiety-provoking situation. This highlights an important aspect of not only the ABC triangle, but CBT in general: how you react is determined not only by the situation, but also by the meaning you assign to the situation.

Let's consider another example. In this case, you're in your house and hear a crashing noise in another room. How you react to the noise will depend at least partially on what you think caused the noise. If you think someone is breaking in, you'd probably get very anxious, and you might phone the police and look for a place to hide. If instead you think your dog knocked something over, you'd have a very different reaction: you'd probably feel annoyed, and you might yell at your dog or get a broom to sweep up the mess.

The important thing to keep in mind is that your reaction is only partly based on the situation. When you first hear the crashing noise, you don't know whether it's someone breaking in, your dog, or perhaps something else. Your emotional reaction, be it fear, annoyance, or a different feeling, is largely based on the meaning you give the situation, or how you interpret it.

EXERCISE 2.1: Looking at How Thoughts Influence Feelings and Behaviors

In order to really understand how the meaning you ascribe to a situation influences your reactions, read through the following examples. Try to come up with different ways of thinking about each of the situations, then consider how those thoughts would influence how you felt and what you did as a result. We've filled in the first example to help you see how this works.

Situation 1: A colleague invites you to a party. He wants you to meet his friends, none of whom you know.

> **Possible thought 1:** *Sounds like fun! I'll get to meet some new people and maybe make some new friends.*
>
> **Feelings:** *Happy and excited*
>
> **Behaviors:** *I go to the party, introduce myself to new people, and talk with them.*
>
> **Possible thought 2:** *That sounds terrible! I won't know anyone, and I'll probably feel awkward the entire time I'm there.*
>
> **Feelings:** *Nervous and anxious*
>
> **Behaviors:** *I call my colleague, make an excuse, and avoid the party. Or I go to the party but hardly speak to anyone and then leave early.*

Situation 2: Your boss tells you she wants to give you a promotion. In your new position, you'll lead a team and work independently.

> **Possible thought 1:** _____
>
> _____
>
> **Feelings:** _____
>
> **Behaviors:** _____
>
> _____
>
> **Possible thought 2:** _____
>
> _____
>
> **Feelings:** _____

Behaviors: _____

_____

Situation 3: You phoned a friend and left a voice mail message. It's been a week, and he hasn't called you back.

Possible thought 1: _____

_____

Feelings: _____

Behaviors: _____

_____

Possible thought 2: _____

_____

Feelings: _____

Behaviors: _____

_____

Situation 4: You made plans with friends to go out for brunch. At the last minute, you find out that the restaurant you were planning to go to misplaced the reservation, so one of your friends made a reservation at another restaurant. The restaurant you're now going to just opened, and you've never eaten there before.

Possible thought 1: _____

_____

Feelings: _____

Behaviors: _____

_____

Possible thought 2: _____

_____

Feelings: _____

Behaviors: _____

_____

What Does CBT Aim to Change?

Because thoughts, feelings, and behaviors influence each other, changing one point of the triangle can lead to changes in the other two points of the triangle. We'll use fear of flying to illustrate this idea. Let's say that you're afraid of flying, but you need to take a plane to attend a friend's wedding. You might have the thought *What if the plane crashes while I'm on it?* This would probably make you anxious and lead you to come up with an excuse about why you can't attend the wedding. Once you avoid having to take the flight, your anxiety would probably decrease, and you'd feel relieved. You might then tell yourself, *Good thing I canceled my travel plans. Even if the plane didn't crash, I probably would have panicked while on the flight.*

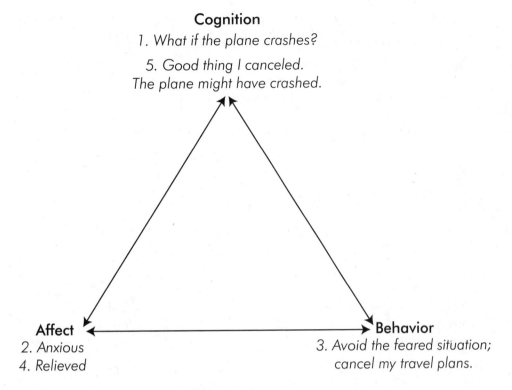

Cognition

1. What if the plane crashes?

5. Good thing I canceled.
The plane might have crashed.

Affect

2. Anxious
4. Relieved

Behavior

3. Avoid the feared situation;
cancel my travel plans.

FIGURE 2.7.

Suppose, however, that instead of avoiding taking the plane and therefore missing the wedding, you decided to try something different. Perhaps you went to the airport a few weeks before your flight and watched the planes take off and land. This would probably make you quite anxious at first, but as the number of flights arriving and departing without incident increased, your anxiety would probably decrease. In addition, you might think, *A lot of planes have passed through this airport and there haven't been any accidents. Maybe my own flight won't be so dangerous.* In this example, both your emotional reaction and your thoughts changed because you changed your behavior.

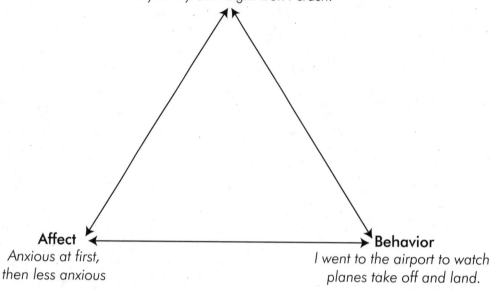

Cognition
All the planes arrived and departed without incident.
Maybe my own flight won't crash.

Affect
Anxious at first,
then less anxious

Behavior
I went to the airport to watch
planes take off and land.

FIGURE 2.8. The impact of changing your behavior.

Another option is that you might instead decide to reevaluate your thinking about the situation. For example, perhaps you'd tell yourself, *I've often heard people say that flying is actually safer than driving a car, so the chances that my plane will crash are pretty slim. Besides, I can't avoid every situation that isn't 100 percent safe because then I'd never do anything.* Assuming that you believe these thoughts, your feelings of anxiety might lessen a bit, and you might decide to keep your travel plans and go to the wedding.

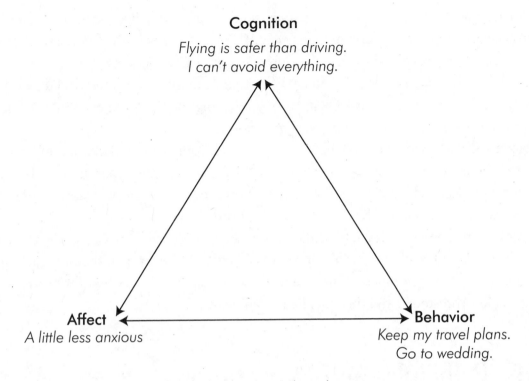

Cognition
Flying is safer than driving.
I can't avoid everything.

Affect
A little less anxious

Behavior
Keep my travel plans.
Go to wedding.

FIGURE 2.9.   The impact of reevaluating your thoughts.

Although you can directly change what you do and reevaluate what you think, it's much more difficult to directly change your emotions. As you probably already know, you can't just decide not to be anxious (if only it were that easy!). And even if you wanted to, you'd probably have to think or do something that would lead to an emotional change; for example, you might try to think of something calming or perhaps do a relaxing activity, such as yoga, in an attempt to make yourself feel less anxious. We can change what we do and learn to change how we think, but it's next to impossible to directly change our feelings. Therefore CBT targets emotions indirectly by focusing instead on recognizing and changing thoughts and behaviors.

Because you can directly influence your thoughts and behaviors but only indirectly influence your emotions, the primary target of CBT for GAD is excessive worry (a thought), not anxiety. This doesn't mean that managing anxiety isn't an important goal. After all, experiencing chronic and excessive anxiety can lead to significant distress and disruption of daily life. Plus, if you don't feel less anxious after using the CBT strategies in this book, you probably won't be satisfied with your progress.

However, since worries are thoughts, whereas anxiety is an emotional (and physical) response, by directly targeting worries you can indirectly decrease your anxiety. In fact, research has clearly shown that reductions in worry levels lead to decreases in anxiety among people who receive CBT for GAD (more on that later in this chapter). Moreover, as discussed in chapter 1, people typically experience anxiety when they perceive a threat. Because worries involve thoughts about potential negative outcomes in the future, they're experienced as threatening and therefore lead to anxiety. As such, when you worry less, you'll feel less threatened and therefore be less anxious.

CBT Principles and Expectations

Before starting CBT, it's important to understand exactly what's expected of you. A commitment of both time and effort is required in order to have maximum success with the strategies described in this workbook. However, before you can agree to put forth the effort, you need to know what you'll be asked to do and why you'll be asked to do it.

Acquiring Skills

A primary goal of CBT is to help people learn skills they can use throughout life to better manage difficult situations, feelings of distress, and problematic thoughts and behaviors. In our clinical practice, we tell our clients that they'll learn how to become their own therapists. This is because one of the roles of a CBT therapist is to help people recognize unhelpful patterns of thinking and behaving and then change those patterns in a way that reduces distress. Learning to become your own therapist therefore means being able to identify the problem and taking effective, healthy action. To that end, CBT helps you build a toolbox of skills. The aim is to learn which tool is right for a given job, and to master the use of each tool so that you can utilize it when needed.

Focusing on the Here and Now

In CBT, the focus is on thoughts, behaviors, and feelings in the present, rather than early childhood experiences or the distant past. This isn't to say you won't consider past events. On the contrary, looking at past patterns and experiences can sometimes be very helpful. For example, if you're very anxious about taking an exam and think, *I'll probably fail*, you might try to challenge this thought by reviewing how you've performed on past exams. In addition, having an understanding of your own personal history with a given fear can often help you place your thoughts in context, which will assist you in challenging problematic thoughts. For example, you might recall that in high school you predicted that you would pass all of your exams, but in fact you failed one of them. You can then see that this past experience probably contributed to your current expectation that you'll fail exams.

So past experiences can provide important information about problematic thoughts and behaviors. However, CBT focuses on the impact of thoughts and behaviors in the present because what might have originally caused a problem is often very different from what's keeping the problem alive. Focusing on the origins of problematic worry and anxiety, while interesting and informative, often isn't enough to help you make changes in the present.

Let's say you have a long-standing fear of needles. Your fear is severe enough that you avoid even looking at needles, including movie scenes with needles or injections, and that you've put off necessary dental procedures because you're afraid of getting an injection. If you decide to investigate the initial cause of this fear, you might find out that when you were young you had a terrible experience with getting a shot at the doctor's office. Perhaps you were crying and trying to avoid the needle and unfortunately got jabbed with it a few times before finally getting the injection. You were so upset at the time that your parents had to hold you down throughout the process. Getting jabbed with the needle was painful and scary, and you've been afraid of needles and injections since. In this case, you've identified the cause of the problem. It's unlikely, however, that simply knowing why you're afraid of needles will reduce your fear in the present or keep you from avoiding situations where you might see a needle or receive an injection. Rather, understanding what's maintaining your fear is likely to be more helpful.

It's important to note that although initial causes aren't emphasized in CBT, this doesn't mean identifying them has no value. Many people enter into therapy because they want to understand the origins of their problems, and this can be both helpful and rewarding. However, that isn't a goal of CBT. When you decide to tackle your anxiety using CBT strategies, you're choosing to focus on the thoughts and behaviors that are maintaining your problem in the present. And when it comes to dealing with anxiety, research suggests that this is by far the most effective strategy.

Engaging in Lots of Practice

CBT involves learning new skills, and practice is crucial for mastering those skills. To that end, every chapter in this workbook includes exercises you need to complete. You'll do some of the exercises several times over the course of days or weeks. For example, in exercise 1.3, we provided a Worry Monitoring Log and encouraged you to record three worries per day for at least a week.

The exercises generally aren't time-consuming or overly difficult. Like most people, you're probably quite busy in your daily life, and we don't want to introduce an additional burden. Rather, the exercises typically involve thinking about something in a new way or trying to act differently in specific situations. And though this can sometimes feel uncomfortable or awkward, the intent isn't for you to feel overwhelmed or afraid.

Why is practice such an important part of CBT? As with any new skill, only through repetition and practice will you see significant improvements in your mastery and confidence with the skills in this book. Physical therapy provides a good analogy. Let's say you started having back problems, so you decided to make weekly appointments with a physical therapist to work on this. Each week, the physical therapist guides you through a series of stretching exercises to help relieve your back pain. If you only do the recommended stretches during your appointments, your progress will be slow at best. If, on the other hand, you practice all of the exercises regularly, you're likely to experience a significant reduction in pain and discomfort.

Recording Your Experience

A final principle of CBT is the importance of tracking your progress. Throughout this workbook, you'll find many forms for recording your findings and experiences when you complete various exercises, including monitoring forms that can be filled out repeatedly. We encourage you to fill them out either in the workbook or on the downloadable versions available at http://www.newharbinger.com/31519, or to record your answers on paper or electronically. If you use a notebook or electronic device, make sure it's easily portable.

Some people like to take detailed notes about the CBT exercises they do, and if this is your preference, go for it! Others are concerned that they won't have the time to write everything down. If that's the case for you, we recommend taking notes that are short and to the point so the process won't be time-consuming. There are several reasons why it's a good idea to keep a record of your CBT work, discussed in the sections that follow.

MEMORY ISN'T TRUSTWORTHY

If you rely on your memory, you're much more likely to forget things or make mistakes. In general, people tend to best remember recent events or things that occur frequently. For example, if you try to recall what you had for lunch two weeks ago, you probably won't remember. But if you had to take a guess, you'd be likely to say whatever you usually have (for example, a sandwich) or what you had most recently (for example, a salad). If you write things down, you won't have to worry about remembering (so as a bonus, you'll have one less thing to worry about!). Keeping records is especially important when you're learning to recognize and identify your thoughts, and having accurate information will enhance your success.

RECORDS HELP YOU RECOGNIZE PATTERNS

It can be difficult to notice patterns in your thoughts or behaviors if you try to keep track of all your thoughts in your head. As just discussed, one issue is that you probably can't remember everything. Another is that thoughts have a tendency to spin and swirl in the mind—something you might have noticed with your worries. Writing things down keeps them clear. You can look at what you've written and see if there's a pattern to what you do or how you think.

TRACKING HELPS YOU SEE YOUR PROGRESS

Another benefit to recording the results of the exercises you do in this book is that it allows you to track your progress. It can be more difficult than you might think to notice when you're actually improving. Most of our clients observe gains in the beginning and are justifiably proud as a result. Gains are relatively easy to observe early in therapy, since the only point of comparison clients have is how they were doing before starting CBT; any gains or improvements are therefore quite noticeable.

However, as time passes and progress continues, it's common for people to start using their ideal outcome as a point of comparison, rather than how they were doing at the start or how far they've progressed along the way. As a result, they see their current status as less than their ideal, rather than as an improvement upon where they once were.

Although it's always a good idea to have goals to strive for, it's important that those goals be realistic and motivating. You don't want them to become a source of feelings of failure. It's like climbing a mountain. You know it will take effort, but you take up the challenge one step at a time. If you look down every once in a while as you're climbing, you can see how far you've come. If, however, you only look up, you might focus simply on the fact that you haven't reached the summit yet, no matter how far you've gone. This can feel demoralizing, and might even make you want to give up and stop climbing. Keeping a written record of what you've accomplished will allow you to see how far you've come without in any way obscuring where you still want to go.

Another reason why tracking your progress is so important is that as you work on CBT skills, you'll probably find that exercises that were initially difficult become quite easy over time. Written records allow you to better recognize this by helping you see what you struggled with in the past and how you're managing in the present. We've seen many of our clients quickly forget how difficult certain tasks used to be for them, and therefore downplay their progress. Because tackling worry and anxiety takes effort, it's important to acknowledge and take pride in all of the gains you make.

A RESOURCE FOR LIFE

A final benefit of keeping written records of your experience is that you can keep your notes for future reference. It's common to have occasional increases in worry and anxiety during stressful times. When this happens, you can manage the resurgence of worry and anxiety quickly by reviewing your notes to determine which strategies have worked well for you in the past.

The fact is, after working your way through this book, you'll be a different person, with new ways of thinking and behaving. People who successfully complete a CBT treatment tend to stay well for very long periods of time if they continue to use the strategies that helped them in the first place. That's why CBT can produce lifelong results.

Research Findings

As mentioned earlier in this chapter, CBT is based on research. The CBT strategies described in this workbook are no exception. Over several decades, our research team has spearheaded many of the studies investigating the nature of GAD and the CBT strategies most effective for treating it. In a number of studies, the treatment approaches described in this book were found to be helpful in reducing GAD symptoms. In addition, one concept associated with GAD—intolerance of uncertainty (discussed in depth in chapter 5)—has been shown to have an especially strong relationship to GAD symptoms and is therefore a key target of treatment.

The CBT strategies in this book were originally developed in the early 1990s at Laval University in Quebec, Canada. Since the development of this CBT protocol, its efficacy has been examined in many clinical trials (for example, Dugas et al. 2010; Gosselin et al. 2006; and Ladouceur et al. 2000). In fact, it has been tested in more clinical trials than any other psychological treatment for GAD. Overall, the findings show that 70 to 80 percent of individuals with GAD who receive this form of CBT in one-on-one sessions with a therapist no longer meet diagnostic criteria for GAD after treatment. In addition, long-term findings from these studies show that the vast majority of those who are successfully treated maintain their treatment gains for periods of at least two years. (Data for longer periods are not yet available.) Thus, approximately 75 percent of people who suffer from GAD can expect to benefit from the strategies described in this book and maintain their gains for extended periods of time.

Having read the preceding paragraph, you might be thinking, *Why do some people not fully benefit from this treatment? How can I ensure the treatment will be helpful for me?* There are no simple answers to these questions. There is, however, one clear predictor of success: motivation to change. The research findings show that being willing to do all the work required to improve is a strong predictor of success in overcoming GAD symptoms. People who are ready to put in the time and effort to learn and apply the treatment strategies described in this book are more likely to benefit from these strategies. The take-home message is that although there are no guarantees (more on that later), you should see a clear relationship between how much time and effort you put into the approaches in this book and how much you benefit from them. So please put your best foot forward.

What to Expect After Finishing This Workbook

Before you dive into the next chapter, we want to give you an idea of what results you can expect if you faithfully apply the strategies in this book. Many clients who enter our clinical practice arrive with the expectation that they will be completely worry-free at the end of treatment. This isn't a realistic expectation. Everyone worries on occasion, and there will be times in your life when worry is absolutely appropriate—for example, if a loved one falls ill. Therefore, we tell our clients that the goal is to manage worry, not eliminate it. This principle also applies to anxiety. A successful outcome won't leave you anxiety-free; that's impossible, given that anxiety is a basic and necessary system in your body, and there are many times when feeling anxious is appropriate. A more realistic goal is to have a toolbox of helpful strategies for managing worry and anxiety when they arise so you won't experience them as excessive or distressing, and so you can work to reduce them in situations where they aren't appropriate.

Beyond this basic goal, we strongly recommend that you give some thought to what else you hope to accomplish as a result of your work with this book. Given that you're reading this book, excessive worry and anxiety are obviously a problem for you, which is why you wish to reduce them. However, an important question to ask yourself is *why*. That is, what things are worry and anxiety preventing you from doing? If you didn't worry so much, how would your life be different? Perhaps you want to spend more time with your children, change careers, or generally be more spontaneous. Because mastering CBT skills for GAD does take some effort, it's important to have goals worth striving for—a carrot that keeps you moving forward. To that end, the next exercise will help you set some life goals.

EXERCISE 2.2: Setting Goals

This exercise is designed to help you set goals for yourself in different areas of life. We encourage you to take the time to think about each of the areas covered. To be clear, we don't expect you to achieve all of the goals you set by the time you finish this workbook. Some of them might be more long-term. Plus, as people progress through CBT for GAD, they often find that their goals change. (If this is the case for you, visit http://www

.newharbinger.com/31519 to download a fresh worksheet for recording your new goals.) The purpose of setting these goals is to remind you why you want to put in the time and effort required to learn CBT strategies for managing your worry and anxiety.

For each of the different areas of life covered in this exercise, ask yourself the following questions:

- Are worry and anxiety preventing me from doing something I'd like to do?

- If I worried less, what would change?

Try to be as concrete as possible. Clear goals are easier to achieve than vague ones. For example, "I'd like to be happy" is vague; it would be hard to know when you've achieved that goal. In contrast, "I'd like to travel more" is a clear, concrete goal.

Work and school (Possible goals include taking on new responsibilities at work, changing jobs, or going back to school.)

_____

_____

_____

Family and home life (Possible goals include spending more time with family or reconnecting with family members.)

_____

_____

_____

Friends and interpersonal relationships (Possible goals include reconnecting with old friends or socializing more.)

_____

_____

_____

Leisure activities and hobbies (Possible goals include traveling more, trying local restaurants, or completing home repairs.)

_____

_____

_____

Personal characteristics (Possible goals include being more spontaneous, being more assertive, or allowing others to make plans sometimes.)

_____

_____

_____

Other goals

_____

_____

_____

CHAPTER 3

Is Worry Helpful?

If you're like many people with GAD, worry is probably something that you've been doing for most of your life. And when you do something for most of your life, it can be hard not to view it as at least a bit useful. Think about all of the positive things that have happened in your life: Did you do well at school? Do you have friends? Do you love and care about someone in your life? Have you succeeded at something important to you? Have you had a job that you liked? Do people in your life think well of you? It's natural to think that worrying about these aspects of your life (education, friendships, love, success, career, and family) has had positive effects on the outcomes you've experienced. And people tend to want to continue doing things that they view as useful and helpful in their lives. For example, if you always review your notes an hour before an exam and you tend to get good grades, you're probably going to continue using this strategy. The same idea applies to worry. If you've been worrying for most of your life, you probably believe that doing so has helped you achieve some of the positive things in your life.

This chapter will discuss beliefs about the benefits of worry. Although the focus of this book as a whole is on strategies to reduce worry, it's important to know whether you believe worry has been helpful in your life. If you do hold such beliefs, it will probably be more difficult than you might expect to let go of your worries.

Do You See Worry as Helpful?

You might be surprised to learn that most people report having some positive beliefs about the benefits of worry, particularly people who have GAD. In fact, research into the beliefs people have about their worry has shown that those with GAD not only report believing that worry is helpful, but also do so to a greater degree than people with moderate worry (Ladouceur et al. 1999).

In this section, we'll help you discover whether you think worry is helpful. Start by writing three of the worries you've had over the past several weeks in the spaces that follow. If you need help identifying recent worries, you can consult your Worry Monitoring Log, from chapter 1. Be specific. Don't write general areas of worry, such as "my family," "my job," or "my health;" instead, write down specific worries, such as "I worry about performing well at work" or "I worry about developing a heart problem later on in life."

Worry 1: _____

_____

Worry 2: _____

_____

Worry 3: _____

_____

Now look at each worry in turn. When you think about it, does it feel like this worry might have helped you or been positive in some way? If you're like many people, you probably think worrying about these topics was at least somewhat useful. A good way to find out whether you have any positive beliefs about the benefits of worry is to ask yourself the following questions about each of the worries you listed:

- What does worrying about this topic say about me or my values?

- If I didn't worry about this topic, what would that say about me or my values?

- What benefit is there to me when I worry about this?

- Does worrying about this topic lead me to act differently than I normally would?

- Am I concerned that something negative might happen if I didn't worry about this topic?

To see how this works, we'll use the thought *I worry about my children's safety when they walk to school by themselves* as an example and go through those questions.

What does worrying about this topic say about me or my values?

Worrying about my children's safety shows that I love them and care about their well-being.

If I didn't worry about this topic, what would that say about me or my values?

It might say that my children's safety isn't a big priority for me and that I'm more concerned about other things.

What benefit is there to me when I worry about this?

When I worry about my children's safety, I feel reassured that I've thought of any and all harm that could come to them, and maybe even prevented something bad from happening to them as a result.

Does worrying about this topic lead me to act differently than I normally would?

Worrying about this topic makes me more vigilant to potential dangers my children might face and allows me to prepare them for these dangers, such as teaching them to look both ways before crossing the street.

Am I concerned that something negative might happen if I didn't worry about this topic?

I'd be concerned that I'd forget to tell them something important about their safety, which could potentially put them in harm's way.

EXERCISE 3.1: Are Your Worries Helpful?

In this exercise, you'll examine one of the worries you listed in the preceding section by answering the same questions. This will help you see whether you have any beliefs about the benefits of your own worries. We highly recommend that you complete this exercise for several of your most common or most problematic worries. To download additional copies of this worksheet, visit http://www.newharbinger.com/31519.

Worry: _____

_____

What does worrying about this topic say about me or my values?

_____

_____

_____

If I didn't worry about this topic, what would that say about me or my values?

_____

_____

_____

What benefit is there to me when I worry about this?

_____

_____

_____

Does worrying about this topic lead me to act differently than I normally would?

_____

_____

_____

Am I concerned that something negative might happen if I didn't worry about this topic?

_____

_____

_____

Looking over your answers, did you find any advantages or benefits to your worries? If you did, you hold positive beliefs about the usefulness of worry. It might seem strange to discuss benefits you believe you may be getting from worry, especially since this workbook is focused on strategies to reduce worry. However, this is actually the very reason you need to recognize your positive beliefs about worry: if you believe worry is helpful in your life, you might find it difficult to let go of your worries.

Common Positive Beliefs About the Usefulness of Worry

In the sections that follow, we'll discuss five of the benefits people most commonly believe they receive from worrying. As you read through these sections, notice whether any of the benefits of worry you listed in the preceding exercise fit into one of these categories.

Belief 1: Worry Is a Positive Personality Trait

People who hold the belief that worry is a positive personality trait see worry as proof that they're good or productive people. If you believe that worry reflects positive character traits, you might think worry shows that you're caring, loving, conscientious, or concerned about others, or that you have excellent attention to detail. Here are a few examples of this belief:

- *Worrying about how my children do at school shows that I'm a caring and loving parent who's concerned about their education.*

- *Worrying about the details of my job shows that I'm conscientious and hardworking.*

- *I show my parents how much I love and care for them when I worry about their health and happiness.*

If you hold this belief, you might even describe yourself to others as a worrier, saying things like "People know that I worry about how everyone is doing" or "I'm the kind of person who won't forget any of the small details of my job; I'm a worrier." In this light, worry is seen as beneficial because it demonstrates a positive aspect of your personality both to yourself and to others.

Belief 2: Worry Helps with Problem Solving

Many people believe that worrying about something helps them deal with whatever they're worrying about more effectively. If you hold this belief, you think worry helps you plan and prepare for different situations or solve problems. Here are a few examples of this belief:

- *If I worry about my problems at work, I'll be more likely to come up with good solutions to those problems.*

- *Worrying about my upcoming vacation will help me better plan and prepare for any problems that might arise on the trip.*

- *Worrying about a home remodeling project allows me to develop the most efficient and cost-effective plan for the renovations.*

If you hold this belief, you see worry as a thought process that helps you think through all aspects of a difficult situation more effectively, sometimes even before anything negative happens. In this light, worry is seen as useful because it can help you not only better deal with your problems and manage them efficiently, but also sometimes avoid problems altogether. For example, if you worry about what to do if it rains while you're on vacation, you may come up with a plan for activities to do no matter what the weather, thereby avoiding difficulties or stress during your vacation.

Belief 3: Worry Provides Motivation

Another common belief about the benefits of worry is that worry can provide motivation to act. If you hold this belief, you probably think that if you worry about something, that means it's important and you will therefore be more likely to deal with the situation. Here are a few examples of this belief:

- *Worrying about my health motivates me to take better care of myself by exercising and eating well.*

- *If I worry about my upcoming exams, it means they're important to me, and I'm likely to study harder.*

- *When I worry about my tasks at work, I'm more likely to get started on them right away and do a good job.*

If you hold this belief, you see worry as something that spurs you into action because it indicates that you're thinking about something important. In this light, worry is seen as helpful because it makes you more likely to do something about a situation that's important to you.

Belief 4: Worry Provides Protection from Negative Emotions

Many people believe worrying about negative events provides emotional preparation should those negative events actually occur. This belief is a bit like looking at worry as "money in the bank": *If I worry about something bad now, I will have already invested time and energy into worrying about it. Then, if the event happens, I'll be more prepared and therefore less upset.* Here are a few examples of this belief:

- *If I worry about the health of my family, I'll feel less upset and overwhelmed if someone in my family actually does get sick.*

- *Worrying about getting fired from my job makes me more able to cope with all the feelings of loss, embarrassment, and fear I'd probably experience if I actually were fired.*

- *If I didn't worry about my partner being in a car accident, I would probably be so devastated if it did happen that I wouldn't be able to handle it.*

If you hold this belief, you see worry as beneficial because it can help you better cope with negative events and all the painful feelings that could result. People with this belief often say they can't even imagine how overwhelmed they would be by sadness, fear, or guilt if they didn't worry beforehand about negative events like losing a loved one or becoming seriously ill. As you may have noticed, this belief also includes the idea that worrying about something shows how important it is to you. For this reason, some people believe they'd feel guilty if something bad had happened and they hadn't worried about it beforehand.

Belief 5: Worry Can Prevent Negative Outcomes

The final belief involves the idea that worry, in and of itself, can prevent bad things from happening. In other words, the act of worrying about something can make it less likely to happen. This is a somewhat superstitious belief, and many people will immediately say they don't believe this. However, we are all prone to some superstitions, whether we are aware of it or not. For example, if you've ever knocked on wood after saying that you or someone you care about is healthy, then you have a superstitious belief that doing this will keep them that way. Think about something important that might have come up recently in your life; maybe you had to give a presentation at work or at school, went to a job interview, or traveled somewhere unfamiliar. You probably worried beforehand, and if things went well, you might have thought it was a good thing that you worried: *If I hadn't worried, I bet that things wouldn't have gone well*, or maybe *Good thing I worried! Everything turned out all right.* Here are a few examples of this belief:

- *If I hadn't worried about my children's happiness and comfort while they were away at camp, they probably would have had a terrible time.*

- *Because I worried about my presentation at work, I did a good job.*

- *Whenever I worry about going on an airplane trip, the flight is always smooth, with no incidents or air turbulence.*

In a nutshell, people who hold this belief think worrying about something has a direct effect on the outcome: either bad things would have happened if they hadn't worried, or good things happened because they did worry. If you believe you get this benefit from worry, you can see how you might view the idea of not worrying as potentially dangerous, since it could lead to negative outcomes.

EXERCISE 3.2: Identifying Your Own Positive Beliefs About the Usefulness of Worry

Now that you're familiar with some of the common beliefs people hold about the benefits of worry, you can investigate whether any of those beliefs have a bearing on your day-to-day worries. This exercise is to be done over several days. When you notice yourself worrying about a particular topic, take a moment to think about whether you see that worry as useful, and if so, whether the benefit fits into one of the five beliefs we've been discussing. If it does, write that specific worry under the belief that you feel best applies to your thoughts about that worry.

If you have difficulty deciding whether you hold beliefs about the benefits of a particular worry, revisit exercise 3.1 and ask yourself the questions there. Also, bear in mind that not everyone holds all five beliefs, so it's okay if you don't have personal examples for each of the following beliefs.

1. Worry Is a Positive Personality Trait

This category includes any beliefs that worry is evidence of a positive aspect of your character or personality.

Do you hold this belief about your worries? Yes _____   No _____

List some examples from your own worries where this belief is involved:

_____

_____

_____

_____

_____

2. Worry Helps Me Problem Solve

This category includes any beliefs that your worries help you better plan and prepare for difficult situations, think about all aspects of a problem, or come up with better solutions.

Do you hold this belief about your worries? Yes _____   No _____

List some examples from your own worries where this belief is involved:

_____

_____

_____

_____

_____

3. Worry Helps Motivate Me

This category includes any beliefs that reflect the idea that worrying about something makes you more likely to act on the situation.

Do you hold this belief about your worries? Yes _____   No _____

List some examples from your own worries where this belief is involved:

_____

_____

_____

_____

_____

4. Worry Protects Me from Negative Emotions

This category includes any beliefs that worrying about bad things that could happen protects you from feeling negative emotions, such as sadness, fear, or guilt, should the event actually occur.

Do you hold this belief about your worries? Yes _____   No _____

List some examples from your own worries where this belief is involved:

_____

_____

_____

_____

_____

5. Worry Can Prevent Negative Outcomes

This category includes any beliefs that worry, in and of itself, can prevent negative outcomes or increase the likelihood of positive outcomes.

Do you hold this belief about your worries? Yes _____   No _____

List some examples from your own worries where this belief is involved:

_____

_____

_____

_____

_____

Acknowledging Ambivalence

By now this chapter might seem a little confusing. When you first started reading this book, it was with the clear intention that you wanted to reduce your worries, and you were probably sure that worry was a negative and disruptive part of your life. But if you recognized some of the beliefs we've been discussing as thoughts you've had about your own worries, you might be feeling that perhaps some of your worries are more helpful to you than you realized. So how is it possible to believe worry is negative while also believing it can be useful? The answer to this lies in how you think about your worries.

When you think about how worrying has had a negative impact on your quality of life, you're thinking about worry in general. That is, you're thinking about the act of worrying as a whole: the process of spinning in your head most of the day, and the negative effects that has on everyday aspects of your life. You aren't thinking about any particular worry. In contrast, beliefs you might have about the benefits or usefulness of worry are related to specific worries. So although you might think that, in general, it isn't helpful to spend your days worrying, you might also think that specific worries—about your health, for example— are quite beneficial because they ensure that you exercise regularly. In this way, you can easily hold negative beliefs about worry overall while still holding positive beliefs about the usefulness of some of your specific worries.

All of that said, it's important to bear in mind that whether we're talking about worrying in general or specific worries, the exact same thought process is involved. And if you're successful at working through all the treatment strategies in this book, you can expect to worry less and get rid of the negative impacts of worry on your life. However, if you see worry as useful, this success may also entail losing the aspects of worry that seem beneficial to you. In other words, you can't get rid of the general process of worry without also getting rid of specific worries. If the idea of worrying less about specific topics seems a bit distressing, you may be ambivalent about moving forward with the strategies in this book. Although a part of you wants to worry less, another part of you may be fearful or reluctant to do so.

If you're like most people, you could have a difficult time acknowledging any reluctance to reduce your worry. Many clients we see initially deny holding positive beliefs about worry, often out of concern that they won't seem ready, willing, and able to dedicate themselves to treatment. Yet ambivalence about worry is actually quite common. After all, if you believe that worry shows that you're a good person, helps you solve problems more effectively, motivates you to take action, helps you better cope with and manage negative emotions, and can even prevent negative things from happening, worrying less can seem like a potentially dangerous or undesirable course of action.

Obviously, simply thinking something doesn't make it so. Therefore, believing that worry is useful doesn't mean it actually is. In the next chapter, we'll help you begin to evaluate whether your worries are, in fact, leading to genuine benefits. But first, let's take a look at the gains and losses you anticipate experiencing if you achieve a significant reduction in your worry.

EXERCISE 3.3: Considering Your Gains and Losses If You Worry Less

This exercise is designed to help you realistically look at what you're hoping to achieve by worrying less, along with what you're fearful of losing if you worry less. The sections for gains and losses are each broken down into various areas of life. Please take the time to consider both the positive and negative impacts that reducing worry will have in each of these areas. We recommend giving yourself at least a week to reflect on this exercise.

Gains in Life If I Worry Less

Impacts on my relationships with friends and family

_____

_____

_____

Impacts on my job or school performance

_____

_____

_____

Impacts on my character or personality

_____

_____

_____

Impacts on my ability to complete daily tasks

_____

_____

_____

Impacts on my leisure activities or downtime

_____

_____

_____

Impacts on my ability to handle stress

_____

_____

_____

Impacts on my general well-being or happiness

_____

_____

_____

Impacts on other areas of life

_____

_____

_____

Losses in Life If I Worry Less

Impacts on my relationships with friends and family

_____

_____

_____

Impacts on my job or school performance

_____

_____

_____

Impacts on my character or personality

_____

_____

_____

Impacts on my ability to complete daily tasks

_____

_____

_____

Impacts on my leisure activities or downtime

_____

_____

_____

Impacts on my ability to handle stress

_____

_____

_____

Impacts on my general well-being or happiness

_____

_____

_____

Impacts on other areas of life

_____

_____

_____

Thinking About a Life Without Worry

Most people with GAD have been worrying excessively for most of their lives. This is probably also the case for you. Perhaps you see yourself as a born worrier or believe you carry the "worry gene." Although the content of your worries has probably changed a great deal over the years, and you may have had periods of greater or lesser worry depending on the stress you were experiencing, worry has probably been a constant companion in your life. So you may wonder what it will really mean to live a life without persistent worry.

Think about the fabric of your days: How much time do you spend worrying? How much of your day is spent trying to manage your worries, perhaps by distracting yourself, keeping busy, or planning and preparing for future outcomes? How often do you talk about your worries with friends, family, or coworkers? Like many people with GAD, you may spend a great deal of your day worrying, coping with worry, thinking about your worries, or talking about them with others. Therefore, worry has not only been a part of your life for a long time but probably also takes up a great deal of your time.

So how does this affect the goal of living a life without worry? You might not have thought much about what your life would look like if you didn't worry excessively, other than to hope that you'd be happier if you were able to just relax and not have negative thoughts constantly spinning in your head. Although being clearheaded and relaxed is typically pleasant, have you given much thought to what else you'd do with your time? That is, if you aren't spending most of your time either worrying or trying to manage your worries, what will you be doing?

Seeing Yourself as a Worry-Free Person

Your identity as an individual is something worth thinking about. If you've always seen yourself or been seen by others as a worrier, who will you be if that is no longer part of your identity? For anyone who has struggled with anxiety and worry for years, looking beyond overcoming the problem and giving some thought to what life would be like without it is a significant step in moving forward. This is particularly important for people with GAD who have always worried. Because they can't remember a time when they didn't worry, a future without worry is an abstract concept—something that they aren't personally familiar with and can only imagine.

To better explain this, we'll use an analogy of breaking a bone in your leg. If you have an accident in which you break your leg, there are many things you either won't be able to do or will have to do quite differently. You won't be able to run, ride a bike, or go hiking. When you walk, you might need crutches, and activities such as taking a shower or getting ready to go to bed become much more complicated. When thinking about what your life will be like after your leg heals, however, you have a point of comparison: you remember how you walked, ran, rode a bike, took a shower, and went to bed before you broke your leg, and after your leg heals, you'll probably return to doing all of these activities as you used to. But what if you'd had a broken leg since birth? You would have become used to walking or taking a shower in a certain way. Then, if years later your leg suddenly healed, you'd have to learn a new way of doing these things. The latter scenario is what people with GAD face. Since you've probably always been a worrier, life without worry is likely to be quite unfamiliar.

Taking Steps Toward a Life Without Worry

Because a life without excessive worry will probably be new to you, it's important to take some time to think about the kind of life you want for yourself if you aren't always busy worrying, and to also think about the kind of person you want to be if you aren't a worrier. All too often, people with GAD have simply given up on certain goals because they seemed too anxiety-provoking and therefore unrealistic. Maybe you've wanted to travel but the idea of going somewhere completely different elicited too many worries. Or maybe you've wanted to learn how to paint with watercolors, but trying something new seemed too scary. Consider any dreams you've set aside as potential future goals for yourself in a life without worry. In terms of your identity, perhaps you'd like to be a more spontaneous person—someone who can wake up on a Saturday morning and make plans for the day on the spur of the moment. Or perhaps you'd like to see yourself as a more relaxed and easygoing person who's able to adjust to unexpected changes in your daily schedule with little to no anxiety.

At this point, you need not have answers about what a life without worry would look like for you. Now is the time to simply think about it and acknowledge that these thoughts might be simultaneously exciting and scary. As mentioned previously, if you've worried your whole life, it can be difficult to imagine living any other way. With this in mind, the following exercise is designed to help you start thinking about a different kind of life—one that isn't dominated by worry.

EXERCISE 3.4: Thinking About a Life Without Worry

This exercise involves writing down some ideas of what you might like to change in your life or add to your life if you worried less. Don't just fill out this exercise and consider it done. Instead, come back to it several times over the next few months whenever a new idea strikes you. Give yourself some time to really think about what you might enjoy doing with your life, including things you've never thought of trying because they seemed too anxiety-provoking.

Also, you don't have to do this exercise alone. You can ask friends and family members about their interests and what they do in their spare time. You can also take some time to observe other people: Are there positive aspects of someone's personality or character that you admire? Are there things that people do (or don't do) that you'd like to incorporate into your own life? Noticing these things in others can be helpful in figuring out what you might like to do differently.

To help you brainstorm some ideas, we've suggested a few areas of life where you might want to make some changes, and we've provided a few examples for each. Feel free to focus on whichever sections are most meaningful for you, or to brainstorm about other aspects of life if you prefer.

Leisure activities and hobbies (Examples: take a salsa class; travel somewhere alone; take tennis lessons with friends)

_____

_____

_____

Relationship with family and friends (Examples: spend more time with family just having fun; allow my kids more independence; accept more invitations to social events; reconnect with old friends)

_____

_____

_____

Completing daily tasks (Examples: delegate household chores to my kids; stop making excessive to-do lists every day)

_____

_____

_____

Time at work or school (Examples: take time for lunch even when there's work left to do; socialize more with coworkers or classmates; take on new projects that I used to avoid; look for a new job)

_____

_____

_____

My personality or character and related changes in behavior (Examples: be more spontaneous, such as by accepting last-minute invitations if I'm available; be more easy-going, such as by not getting upset if plans change unexpectedly)

_____

_____

_____

CHAPTER 4

Positive Beliefs About Worry: Examining the Evidence

In the previous chapter, we discussed the importance of recognizing any positive beliefs you might have about the usefulness of worry. In this chapter, we'll focus on challenging those beliefs by looking at the evidence and directly investigating whether worry is in fact beneficial.

If you're like most people with GAD, you probably identified a number of positive beliefs about the benefits of worry. At this point, you might think that perhaps reducing worry isn't such a great goal. However, your beliefs about the usefulness of worry may not be accurate. Therefore, it's important to look at the whole picture and investigate whether worry is actually providing you with the benefits you think it is.

Before we begin, we want to be clear about something: the goal of challenging positive beliefs about the function of worry is not to prove you wrong. We don't know whether your worries are actually helpful or not, and no one can, since no one walks in your shoes other than you. However, without examining the evidence, you also can't be sure whether your worries have positive functions. As such, the goal of challenging beliefs about worry is to investigate whether your worries actually provide you with benefits: Do your worries truly reflect positive character traits? Do they actually aid you in problem solving, motivate you, and protect you from negative emotions or negative events? By gathering evidence from your own life, you can begin to answer these questions and decide whether worry is truly a useful or desirable strategy for you.

Putting Your Worries on Trial

A good way to begin challenging the usefulness of worry is to take your worries to court, so to speak. Holding a trial for your worries gives you an opportunity to examine all the evidence for and against the benefits of specific worries. In essence, you'll take on three roles:

- **Defense attorney:** In this role, you'll present a case attempting to prove the value or usefulness of a particular worry.

- **Prosecuting attorney:** In this role, you'll argue against the benefits of the worry, providing evidence that might contradict your positive beliefs about worry.

- **Judge:** In this final role, you'll review the evidence in its entirety and decide whether you are, in fact, receiving the benefits from worry that you initially identified.

As discussed in chapter 3, many people with GAD report that they find worry in general to be negative. The process of spinning in one's head and all the physical symptoms that worry can lead to, such as anxiety, sleep problems, and muscle tension, are viewed as undesirable. However, specific worries are often seen differently. You too may feel that overall worry isn't helpful while still seeing specific worries as more helpful. Perhaps worry about your health feels useful because it ensures that you take good care of yourself, or worrying about your friends and family members seems positive because it shows how much you care about them. These kinds of specific worries are what you'll be investigating. This chapter includes a number of worksheets to aid you in the process of putting a given worry on trial. All are available for download at http://www.newharbinger .com/31519 so that you can take this approach for additional worries.

EXERCISE 4.1: Examining "Helpful" Worries and Positive Beliefs

In this exercise you'll list a few of the specific worries that you identified as helpful in exercise 3.1 and your positive beliefs about each one. Keep in mind that you can hold more than one positive belief about the usefulness of a particular worry. As a reminder, five of the most common positive beliefs about worry are as follows:

1. Worry is a positive personality trait.

2. Worry helps me problem solve.

3. Worry helps motivate me.

4. Worry protects me from negative emotions.

5. Worry can prevent negative outcomes.

We'll begin with an example in case that's helpful.

Worry: *I worry about getting all the household bills paid on time and still having some money in savings.*

Positive beliefs

1. **Worry is a positive personality trait:** *Worrying about the family finances shows that I'm a conscientious and organized person.*

2. **Worry helps me problem solve:** *Worrying about the family finances helps me figure out the best way to manage our money so our bills are paid but we still have money in the bank.*

3. **Worry motivates me:** *Worrying about the family finances ensures that I stay motivated to keep track of all the bills and develop a long-term savings plan.*

Now give it a try for three worries of your own.

Worry: _____

_____

Positive beliefs

1. _____

_____

2. _____

_____

3. _____

_____

Worry: _____

_____

Positive beliefs

1. _____

_____

2. _____

_____

3. _____

_____

Worry: _____

_____

Positive beliefs

1. _____

_____

2. _____

_____

3. _____

_____

The Defense Attorney: Building a Case for Worry

Once you've identified some of the worries you have that strike you as beneficial, you can begin developing a case in defense of them, listing the evidence that supports your belief. There are a number of helpful questions you can ask yourself about your worry. In the sections that follow, we'll outline useful questions for each of the five common beliefs and provide examples. Then we'll provide an exercise that allows you to take this same approach with one of your own worries.

Worry Is a Positive Personality Trait

Example: *Worrying about my children's safety shows that I'm a good and loving parent.*

Do I have examples of times when this worry led me to act in a positive manner?

On several occasions I worried about the potential dangers of my children playing outside alone. Because of this, I'm always with them when they play outside. This reflects that I'm a loving and concerned parent.

Have other people told me that my worries about this topic are positive?

Many of my friends and family members have told me how devoted I am to my children.

Have others acted in a way that demonstrates that this worry is a positive aspect of my personality?

Many of the other parents in our neighborhood trust me to keep an eye on their kids.

Other parents have asked me for advice about taking care of their kids.

Worry Helps with Problem Solving

Example: *Worrying about my tasks at work allows me to anticipate problems and solve them more efficiently.*

Are there specific situations in which this worry helped me figure out or solve a problem?

Last week my boss asked me to take over a complex project. Because I worried about it a great deal, I was able to come up with a good plan for completing the project. If I hadn't worried, I probably would have had a hard time dealing with this new project.

Do I have examples of times when I was more prepared to solve a difficult situation because I worried?

When I'm given a new task, I often worry about anything that could go wrong. On a few occasions problems with a task did arise, and because I had worried about it ahead of time, I was able to quickly come up with a solution.

I tend to worry about most of the projects taking place in my company, not just the ones I oversee. Several times my colleagues have asked me to solve problems they were having with their own projects. Because I worried beforehand about anything that could go wrong, I was able to quickly come up with solutions to help my colleagues.

Worry Provides Motivation

Example: *Worrying about my exams motivates me to study and do well in school.*

Do I have examples of times when this worry motivated me to act? Are there things I might not have done had I not worried?

This semester I was worried about passing my chemistry final. Because of this, I developed a study plan a month before the exam.

I set aside at least two hours every day to study because of my worries about doing well in school.

Worry Provides Protection from Negative Emotions

Example: *Worrying about the health of my loved ones prepares me to deal with sadness and pain if anything bad should happen to them.*

Do I have examples of times when this worry helped me cope with a difficult situation?

Last year my father underwent heart surgery. Because I had worried about my father getting ill or needing surgery, I was better able to cope when I saw him in the hospital. I probably wouldn't have been able to carry on with daily life and go to work if I hadn't worried about this happening.

Do I have examples of times when I felt more prepared to deal with negative feelings because I worried?

My sister got into a car accident last month and was in the hospital for over a week. I think I would have been devastated by it if I hadn't worried about her health and safety before the accident.

Worry Can Prevent Negative Outcomes

Example: *Every time I worry about my husband when he's traveling for work, he comes home safe and sound.*

Do I have examples of times when good things happened because I worried about this?

Last month my husband had to fly to Montreal and then to Chicago for business. I worried about his safety during all of his flights. Because I worried, nothing bad happened and he arrived safely at all of his destinations.

Do I have examples of times when bad things happened because I didn't worry?

A few months ago my husband had to drive out of town for work, and while coming home he got a flat tire. I didn't know he was taking that day trip. If I'd had a chance to worry about the trip beforehand, he probably wouldn't have had a flat tire.

EXERCISE 4.2: Building a Defense for Your Worries

Using your own personal experiences, you can now begin to list evidence in support of the benefits of your worries. Taking one of the worries you listed in exercise 4.1, use the questions in this exercise to help you come up with supporting evidence.

All of the preceding questions for the five common worry beliefs are provided in this exercise. Answer as many or as few as you wish, and feel free to skip those that don't seem relevant to your beliefs about your worry. Also, please note that the questions provided are intended to be a useful tool. However, you can list anything that, in your view, provides evidence for the helpfulness of your worries.

Worry: _____

_____

Evidence That My Worry Is Useful

Worry Is a Positive Personality Trait

Do I have examples of times when this worry led me to act in a positive manner?

_____

_____

_____

Have other people told me that my worries about this topic are positive?

_____

_____

_____

Have others acted in a way that demonstrates that this worry is a positive aspect of my personality?

_____

_____

_____

Worry Helps with Problem Solving

Are there specific situations in which this worry helped me figure out or solve a problem?

_____

_____

_____

Do I have examples of times when I was more prepared to solve a difficult situation because I worried?

_____

_____

_____

Worry Provides Motivation

Do I have examples of times when this worry motivated me to act? Are there things I might not have done had I not worried?

_____

_____

_____

Worry Provides Protection from Negative Emotions

Do I have examples of times when this worry helped me cope with a difficult situation?

_____

_____

_____

Do I have examples of times when I felt more prepared to deal with negative feelings because I worried?

_____

_____

_____

Worry Can Prevent of Negative Outcomes

Do I have examples of times when good things happened because I worried about this?

_____

_____

_____

Do I have examples of times when bad things happened because I didn't worry?

_____

_____

_____

Other Evidence in Defense of This Worry

_____

_____

_____

The Prosecuting Attorney: Building a Case Against Worry

Now that you've presented the case in defense of the usefulness of your worries, you can start to look at the other side of the coin. In this section, we'll explore the types of evidence that argue against beliefs that worry is helpful. Again, we'll outline useful questions for each of the five common beliefs. To really clarify the process, we'll use the same example for each belief. Then we will once again provide an exercise for examining one of your own worries in the same way.

Worry Is a Positive Personality Trait

Example: *Worrying about my children's safety shows that I'm a good and loving parent.*

Is there any evidence that I've displayed this positive personality trait without having worried beforehand?

I sometimes do things to protect my children's safety without having previously worried about it. For example, I hold their hands when we cross the street and strap on their seat belts as soon as we get in the car.

Do I know someone with this positive trait who doesn't worry? If so, how does that person show this trait?

One of my neighbors is a great parent. She's very loving and caring toward her son, and she definitely isn't someone who worries a lot. She shows this trait by her actions. I see her being affectionate with her son, and I also see that she cares for his safety. She seems to do many of the things I do, just without worrying about them as much.

Have I ever seen my worry as a negative personality trait?

I sometimes find that I don't enjoy my time with my children. Often I'm so preoccupied with my worries that when I'm with them I may be impatient or irritable, rather than loving and caring.

Have others ever told me that my worry is a negative personality trait?

My children have told me that I often seem preoccupied or distracted and that they find it annoying.

My husband sometimes dismisses my concerns about the kids and says I'm just a worrier. When he says this, I know he doesn't mean it positively.

Worry Helps with Problem Solving

Example: *Worrying about my tasks at work allows me to anticipate problems and solve them more efficiently.*

Do I actually solve my problems when I worry, or do I simply go over them in my head? That is, am I confusing a thought (worry) with an action (problem solving)?

Most of my worries about problems at work aren't about actual problems; they're about potential problems and their negative consequences.

Although I spend a lot of time worrying about how to deal with problems, I don't always seem to solve them.

Has worrying about my problems ever interfered with my ability to solve them? Have I ever procrastinated or avoided dealing with problems because of worry?

Several times I've gotten so worried and anxious about problems at work that I actually avoided dealing with the situation. I also sometimes procrastinate or ask someone else to deal with the situation.

Last week I got so preoccupied with worry about potential work problems that I fell behind on some of my tasks and missed a deadline.

Worry Provides Motivation

Example: *Worrying about my exams motivates me to study and do well in school.*

Do I know people who are motivated and don't worry excessively?

A friend of mine gets excellent grades, and he doesn't worry excessively. He develops a study schedule for his exams, completes all assigned readings, and attends all of his classes.

Has this worry ever interfered with my ability to accomplish things?

I had a difficult time studying for my last exam. I was so worried about failing that I had a hard time concentrating while reading my notes.

Do I ever avoid or put off doing things I'm worried about, rather than becoming motivated to do them?

I sometimes procrastinate on writing class papers because I get anxious when I think about writing them and not doing a good job.

I was so worried about not doing well in my chemistry class that I ended up withdrawing from the course.

Worry Provides Protection from Negative Emotions

Example: *Worrying about the health of my loved ones prepares me to deal with sadness and pain if anything bad should happen to them.*

Did something bad ever happen in the realm of this worry? If so, did I really feel less upset because I'd worried about it?

When my father was in the hospital after his heart attack, I was terrified that he wouldn't make it. I don't think I was really less upset for having worried about his health.

Did something bad ever happen in this realm that I hadn't worried about beforehand? If so, was I able to handle the situation and cope emotionally even though I hadn't worried?

A few years ago, my sister twisted her ankle when she fell down some stairs in my home. I hadn't thought to worry about this beforehand. Although I was really upset and not quite sure what to do, I was able to take care of the situation. I called the paramedics and helped her lie on the couch with her foot resting on a cushion until they arrived. Overall, I think I kept a clear head and dealt with the situation well.

In my daily life, how do I feel emotionally when I worry about bad things that could happen?

When members of my family go on vacation, I'm often anxious and nervous the entire time they're gone because I'm worried something will happen to them while they're away. I also get nervous and worried if anyone in my family is late or if I can't reach them on the phone. Because of this, I'm often quite tense and on edge, even though nothing bad has happened. It's exhausting to feel like this so frequently.

Worry Can Prevent Negative Outcomes

Example: *Every time I worry about my husband when he's traveling for work, he comes home safe and sound.*

Do I have examples of times when bad things happened even though I worried about them?

My husband flew to San Francisco for business a few weeks ago. Even though I worried about him during his trip, he came home with a terrible cold.

Do I have examples of times when good things happened even though I didn't worry?

On several occasions my husband has gone on unexpected day trips for his job. When I don't know about these trips, I'm unable to worry about them, but these trips are usually safe and problem-free.

EXERCISE 4.3: Building a Case Against Your Worries

Taking an approach similar to that in exercise 4.2, you can now start listing evidence against the helpfulness of your worries. Use the same worry as in the previous exercise and build your case against it with examples from your own personal experience.

All of the preceding questions for the five common worry beliefs are provided in this exercise. Again, you can use them to help you challenge your positive beliefs about worry, but feel free to come up with your own questions or to skip any that don't seem relevant to your own beliefs about a particular worry.

Worry: _____

_____

Evidence That My Worry Is Unhelpful

Worry Is a Positive Personality Trait

Is there any evidence that I've displayed this positive personality trait without having worried beforehand?

_____

_____

_____

Do I know someone with this positive trait who doesn't worry? If so, how does that person show this trait?

_____

_____

_____

Have I ever seen my worry as a negative personality trait?

_____

_____

_____

Have others ever told me that my worry is a negative personality trait?

_____

_____

_____

Worry Helps with Problem Solving

Do I actually solve my problems when I worry, or do I simply go over them in my head? That is, am I confusing a thought (worry) with an action (problem solving)?

_____

_____

_____

Has worrying about my problems ever interfered with my ability to solve them? For example, have I ever procrastinated or avoided dealing with problems because of worry?

_____

_____

_____

Worry Provides Motivation

Do I know people who are motivated and don't worry excessively?

_____

_____

_____

Has this worry ever interfered with my ability to accomplish things?

_____

_____

_____

Do I ever avoid or put off doing things that I'm worried about, rather than becoming motivated to do them?

_____

_____

_____

Worry Provides Protection from Negative Emotions

Did something bad ever happen in the realm of this worry? If so, did I really feel less upset because I'd worried about it?

_____

_____

_____

Did something bad ever happen in this realm that I hadn't worried about beforehand? If so, was I able to handle the situation and cope emotionally even though I hadn't worried?

_____

_____

_____

In my daily life, how do I feel emotionally when I worry about bad things that could happen?

_____

_____

_____

Worry Can Prevent Negative Outcomes

Do I have examples of times when bad things happened even though I worried about them?

_____

_____

_____

Do I have examples of times when good things happened even though I didn't worry?

_____

_____

_____

General Challenges Against the Usefulness of Worry

Have my worries about this topic had a negative impact on my relationship with family and friends?

_____

_____

_____

Have my worries about this topic affected my work or school performance?

_____

_____

_____

Has there been an emotional or other toll on me because of my worries about this topic, such as stress or fatigue?

_____

_____

_____

How much time and energy have I spent worrying about this topic?

_____

_____

_____

Other Evidence Against This Worry

_____

_____

_____

The Judge: Weighing the Evidence

In this section, you'll take on the role of judge. In this role, you can look at the evidence as a whole and determine whether your worries are actually as helpful as they seem. Remember that the goal of this exercise is *not* to prove that your beliefs are wrong. Instead, the purpose is to look at your thoughts about worry and decide whether those thoughts are completely accurate.

One of the benefits of generating evidence both for and against a belief is that it allows you to see things that you might not ordinarily notice, including the presence of paradoxes. Many of our clients are surprised to discover that they often list opposing, or paradoxical, pieces of evidence. Let's take a look at some paradoxes from the examples earlier in this chapter.

Example: *Worrying about my children's safety shows that I'm a good and loving parent.*

Evidence for this belief

Many of my friends and family members have told me how devoted I am to my children.

Evidence against this belief

My children have told me that I often seem preoccupied or distracted and that they find it annoying.

My husband sometimes dismisses my concerns about the kids and says I'm just a worrier. When he says this, I know he doesn't mean it positively.

Paradox

The evidence suggests that although being seen as the worrier can be positive, it is also often negative.

Example: *Worrying about my exams motivates me to study and do well in school.*

Evidence for this belief

I set aside at least two hours every day to study because of my worries about doing well in school.

Evidence against this belief

I had a difficult time studying for my last exam. I was so worried about failing that I had a hard time concentrating while reading my notes.

I sometimes procrastinate on writing class papers because I get anxious when I think about writing them and not doing a good job.

Paradox

The evidence suggests that worry can sometimes make me study hard, but it also makes it more difficult for me to do well by affecting my concentration and leading me to put off completing assignments.

As you can see from these examples, it's quite common to have contradictory evidence for the same belief. Similar to the first example, you might find that sometimes you're praised by others for being a worrier, but at other times your concerns are dismissed because you're a worrier. So being a worrier is sometimes positive and sometimes negative. In weighing out the evidence, contradictory experiences that support opposing arguments may suggest that worry isn't as helpful as you originally thought.

EXERCISE 4.4: Finding Paradoxes Within the Evidence

Take some time now to look through what you wrote in exercises 4.2 and 4.3 to see whether there's any contradictory evidence for a particular belief. Keep in mind that paradoxes won't always be present. This exercise is just one part of weighing all the evidence for and against the usefulness of your worries.

Worry: _____

_____

Evidence for this belief

_____

_____

_____

Evidence against this belief

_____

_____

_____

Paradox

_____

_____

_____

Evaluating the Pros and Cons of Worry

Whenever you're considering an important decision, you probably think about the advantages and disadvantages of your choices beforehand. The same can be done with determining the potential usefulness of worry. After all, if you're going to put forth the effort to reduce your worries, it should be based on a clear understanding that you'll gain significantly more in your life by not worrying than you would if you continue to worry.

To explore this, we'll use the previous example of worries about tasks at work and whether they promote effective problem solving.

ADVANTAGES OF WORRYING ABOUT THIS TOPIC

- *By worrying about tasks at work, I can anticipate problems that might arise and plan potential solutions: I therefore have the advantage of being prepared ahead of time.*

- *Worrying about this topic has often led me to think about every aspect of a particular job. My boss and coworkers have told me that I have a great eye for detail. Being seen as a conscientious and detail-oriented person is an advantage of this worry.*

- *Worrying about my tasks at work makes me feel like I'm a good employee who takes the job seriously.*

DISADVANTAGES OF WORRYING ABOUT THIS TOPIC

- *I often spend hours worrying about potential problems at work that never actually happen. Wasting time in this way is a significant disadvantage.*

- *I sometimes get so worked up thinking about potential problems at work that I have hard time concentrating and paying attention to the work I'm doing. Some of my colleagues have noticed this and told me that I need to relax and worry less.*

- *My worries cause me significant anxiety and have sometimes led me to procrastinate or avoid working on certain things. These behaviors can actually make me fall behind in my work.*

OUTCOME OF ADVANTAGES VS. DISADVANTAGES

Once you've listed the pros and cons, you can then weigh them and decide on the value of continuing to worry about a particular topic. In this example, although worrying about work tasks has the advantage of garnering this person praise from colleagues, helping the person be prepared for unlikely problems, and helping the person feel like a good employee, these advantages come at a high physical and emotional cost because the person experiences significant anxiety, distress, and concentration and attention problems, and also wastes a lot of time. In addition, worrying about this topic seems to have the paradoxical effect of interfering with work productivity due to procrastination and avoidance, and colleagues have even commented that the person needs to relax and worry less. Therefore this person might decide that the disadvantages of worry about tasks at work are greater than the advantages.

EXERCISE 4.5: Weighing the Pros and Cons

Continuing in your role as judge, write out a list of the advantages and disadvantages of the worry you've been examining. Use your answers from the previous exercises in this chapter, including your general challenges to worry beliefs (for example, the impact worry has had on your social life and work or school performance, as well as the time, effort, and physical or emotional cost of worry).

Worry: _____

_____

Advantages of worrying about this topic

_____

_____

_____

_____

_____

Disadvantages of worrying about this topic

_____

_____

_____

_____

_____

Reaching a Verdict

For your final act as judge, you need to weigh all of the evidence for and against your belief about the usefulness of this particular worry. This includes your list of all the evidence supporting your belief that the worry is helpful, the evidence against that belief, any paradoxes you identified, and the advantages and disadvantages of this worry. You might also want to include the overall gains and losses associated with worrying less that you listed in exercise 3.3. Then you can review all of the evidence and ask yourself two key questions:

- Is my belief about the usefulness of this worry accurate?

- Does this worry actually benefit me in my life?

Obviously, that's a lot of information to consider. Providing a full example would be lengthy and repetitive, so here we'll give a somewhat streamlined one.

Example: *Worrying about the health of my loved ones prepares me to deal with sadness and pain if anything bad should happen to them.*

Evidence in support of this belief

I felt better able to cope with my father's heart surgery because I worried about his health beforehand.

When my sister was in the hospital after her car accident, I think I would have been devastated if I hadn't worried about her health and safety before the accident.

Evidence against this belief

When my father was in the hospital after his heart attack, I was terrified that he wouldn't make it. I don't think I was really less upset for having worried about his health.

After my sister twisted her ankle when she fell down some stairs in my home, I was able to keep a clear head and cope well with the situation even though I hadn't worried about it before it happened.

When family members are late or away on vacation, I'm often anxious and nervous the whole time they're gone because I'm worried something will happen to them. Because of this, I'm often quite tense and worried, even though nothing bad has happened.

Paradoxes

Although I feel better able to cope with negative events when I worry about them beforehand, I have evidence to the contrary. I also have evidence that I'm probably just as upset about a negative event whether or not I worried about it first.

Advantages to this worry

If I didn't worry about bad things happening to my loved ones, I'd feel guilty.

I can give my family suggestions about ways to ensure their safety because I worry about potential negative events before they happen.

I believe my family knows how much I love them because I worry about them so much.

Disadvantages to this worry

I spend a lot of time thinking about all sorts of bad things that could happen to my family. It's very upsetting, and I often get so anxious that I can't focus on whatever I'm doing at the time.

My family members are sometimes annoyed with me. I call them a lot to check up on them, and I ask them to contact me frequently when they're out of town. They've said that this is very frustrating for them.

I rarely go on vacation because whenever I go I tend to be so worried about my loved ones at home that I can't enjoy my trip.

Outcome (advantages vs. disadvantages)

Although I feel guilty if I don't worry about my loved ones and I think my worry gives me a chance to think ahead, the disadvantages seem to outweigh the advantages. I want my family to know that I love them, but they're often frustrated with me. Plus, I can't enjoy myself when I'm away from them. Also, it's very upsetting to think about bad things that could happen to my loved ones. Because of this, the disadvantages of worrying about this topic outweigh the advantages.

Verdict:

Is my belief about the usefulness of this worry accurate?

No, my belief that worrying about my family protects me from negative emotions isn't completely accurate. When I review the evidence for and against this belief, I can see that I've been quite upset about negative events even when I worried about them, and I also have experience in coping with difficult situations without having worried first.

Does this worry actually benefit me in my life?

No, it comes at a high cost. Although I think I'd feel guilty if I didn't worry, I don't like frustrating my family members with repeated check-ins. Also, I'm frequently anxious, and it's very upsetting to imagine all sorts of terrible scenarios that could happen to my loved ones. Because of these worries, I don't get to enjoy my life, and I don't allow my loved ones to fully enjoy their lives.

EXERCISE 4.6: Reaching Your Own Verdict

Now it's your turn. In the space provided, summarize the main arguments and evidence that you developed throughout this chapter so you can reach a conclusion about the usefulness and benefits of your own worry.

Worry: _____

_____

Evidence in support of this belief

_____

_____

_____

_____

_____

_____

_____

Evidence against this belief

_____

_____

_____

_____

_____

_____

Paradoxes

_____

_____

_____

Advantages to this worry

_____

_____

_____

_____

_____

Disadvantages to this worry

_____

_____

_____

_____

_____

_____

Outcome (advantages vs. disadvantages)

_____

_____

_____

_____

_____

_____

Verdict:

Is my belief about the usefulness of this worry accurate?

_____

_____

_____

_____

_____

_____

_____

Does this worry actually benefit me in my life?

_____

_____

_____

_____

_____

_____

_____

Reviewing Your Verdict

What did you learn from the exercises in this chapter? Did you discover that your worries aren't helpful at all and that there are strong benefits to no longer worrying? Perhaps you found that your worries aren't quite as useful as you thought, but you still believe there's some value to your worries and you're reluctant to let them go. The good news is that whatever you learned about your worries and their perceived usefulness is helpful, as it can guide you in the next steps toward addressing them.

If your worries aren't useful: If the exercises in this chapter allowed you to discover that your worries aren't very helpful, knowing this can reduce any ambivalence you have about letting go of them. Remember, as long as you view worry as a useful strategy, it will be difficult to work toward worrying less.

If your worries are useful: If after challenging your beliefs you found that your worries have some benefits or positive value, it will be important for you to work on finding alternative ways to get the benefits you're currently receiving from worry. In other words, how can you be a good person, an effective problem solver, motivated, and able to cope with negative events without worry? In fact, regardless of whether or not you view your worries as helpful, you might be able to keep the benefits of worry without the actual worry.

One last consideration in regard to the exercises in this chapter: Like most people with GAD, you might find that you have more than one belief about the usefulness of your worries, and that there are several different topics that seem particularly helpful to worry about. Remember, you've probably been worrying for most of your life, so it wouldn't be surprising if you've found many of your worries helpful for several different reasons. Because of this, we encourage you to complete the exercises in this chapter on an ongoing basis, choosing different worries and different beliefs. (As a reminder, all of the worksheets are available for download at http://www.newharbinger.com/31519.) If you find that you're struggling with the idea of letting a particular worry go, come back to these exercises as often as you like.

Moving on to the Next Step

Now that you've completed the work involved in challenging your beliefs about one of your worries, you might be asking yourself, *What now?* The remainder of this workbook will focus on specific strategies you can use to manage and ultimately reduce your worries. However, reevaluating your beliefs about the usefulness of worry will be an ongoing process. We don't expect that you've completely changed your mind about the positive aspects of worry at this point. Rather, we hope this chapter planted a seed. We imagine that, now that you're armed with the knowledge of how you can look at the entire picture of how your worries actually influence your daily life, you'll continue to gather evidence for and against your beliefs. In this way, the seed planted in this chapter will grow naturally with time and your ongoing experience.

Mourning the Loss of Worry

Many of our clients are struck by how emotional the process of challenging their beliefs about worry can be. As mentioned in chapter 3, worry is something that has probably been a constant companion throughout your life, and letting it go can be quite difficult. On the other hand, you might be feeling sad or upset about all the time you've wasted or all the experiences you've missed out on because of worry. Either way, these feelings are absolutely normal, and it's okay to let yourself feel a sense of loss. For some people, this can feel like a period of mourning, both for yourself and for the life you had before you decided to change things. Allow yourself to have these feelings, but as soon as you're ready, move on to chapter 5 so you can start building a different life for yourself—one that's free of excessive worry.

CHAPTER 5

Worry and the Threat of Uncertainty

When we introduced anxiety disorders in chapter 1, we discussed how the theme of threat is what distinguishes the different disorders. This is because anxiety feels like anxiety (for example, racing heart, sweating, or butterflies in the stomach) regardless of the anxiety disorder. So whatever sets off anxiety in the first place is the factor that allows mental health professionals to determine the particular disorder a person is struggling with. For example, if a person has social anxiety, the theme of threat is probably a fear of being negatively evaluated by others. You may wonder what the theme of threat is for GAD. Unlike most anxiety disorders, where there's a clear theme to the threat, what sets off anxiety in GAD is less obvious.

If you have GAD, you probably worry about the same things that everyone else does, you just do so to a much greater extent. In addition, the things you worry about can change from day to day. For example, you might worry about work one day, and the next day you might be more worried about your finances or your health. Although these worries may seem unrelated, they do have a unifying theme: the threat of uncertainty.

An Allergy to Uncertainty

A great number of studies have found that people with GAD are intolerant of uncertainty (see Koerner and Dugas 2006, and Dugas and Robichaud 2007, for a review). People vary greatly in how much uncertainty they can tolerate in their daily lives, but those with GAD can hardly tolerate it at all. For example, someone who can tolerate a great deal of uncertainty might be all right with terminating an apartment lease before finding another place to live. For those with GAD, on the other hand, any situation where there isn't 100 percent certainty about the outcome is likely to be seen as threatening and unacceptable.

In general, people who don't worry excessively tend to have a higher threshold for at least some uncertainty in their lives. For example, if they're going to a friend's house for a dinner party, they probably aren't 100 percent sure they'll enjoy themselves. For them, the small amount of uncertainty in this situation is probably tolerable. In contrast, people with GAD are likely to find the dinner party somewhat threatening because of the uncertainty of the situation.

A good way to think of intolerance to uncertainty is as an allergy. If you're allergic to pollen, it takes only a very small amount of pollen for you to have a strong reaction. You'll probably cough and sneeze, and your eyes will water and itch. The same thing happens with GAD: if you're exposed to even a small amount of uncertainty, you're likely to have a strong reaction. With GAD, that reaction is to feel anxious and worry excessively.

The Worry Cycle

As mentioned in chapter 1, worry is triggered by three types of situations:

- **Unpredictable situations**, where the outcome is unclear (for example, going to the doctor's to get the results of a medical test)

- **Novel situations**, where you're experiencing something completely new to you (for example, trying a new restaurant or starting a new job)

- **Ambiguous situations**, where the situation itself isn't very well-defined (for example, your boss asks to speak with you about your work)

All of these situations have one thing in common: you can't be sure what will happen. Therefore, the outcome of the situation and how you'll handle it are both uncertain. Because of this, you're likely to attempt to mentally plan and prepare, resulting in worry about all of the negative things that could potentially happen.

Here's an example: Suppose you're invited to take a dance class with some friends. If you've never been to a dance class before, this is a novel situation, and therefore likely to lead to worry and anxiety, as illustrated in figure 5.1.

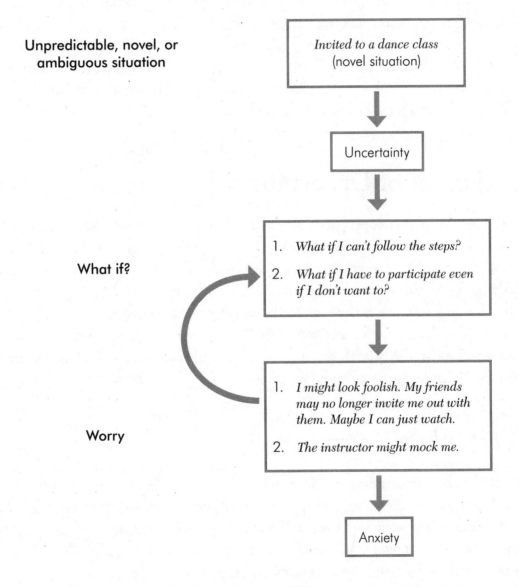

FIGURE 5.1. How uncertainty leads to worry in GAD.

Everyone gets caught up in this kind of worry cycle on occasion. However, given that you have GAD, it's likely that you get caught up in this cycle many times a day, most every day. This happens because uncertainty is inherent in daily life. You can't predict the future, so there will always be situations that you don't expect, that are new to you, or that have unclear elements. You can't be sure whether family or friends from out of town will suddenly show up for a visit, whether you'll be asked to work on a new project for your job, or whether your landlord will be making some renovations to your home. If you have an allergy to uncertainty, you'll react with worry whenever you encounter these kinds of unpredictable, novel, or ambiguous situations.

Given that these situations are an inescapable part of daily life, you may wonder why everyone doesn't worry excessively. The reason people with GAD worry more than others is because they have a negative reaction to uncertainty in day-to-day situations, which turns those situations into threats to be dealt with.

The Threat of Uncertainty

As mentioned in chapter 2, people's reactions to situations are largely determined by how they interpret or think about those situations. For example, if you think air travel is dangerous, you'll probably be very anxious if you're asked to take a flight. However, if you think flying is safe, you won't be anxious and might, in fact, be excited to be taking a trip. In both cases, the situation is the same; only the interpretation differs.

For people with GAD, encountering unpredictable, novel, or ambiguous situations isn't the problem. Rather, the issue is that the uncertainty in these situations is seen as threatening; this is what leads to worry and anxiety.

Beliefs About Uncertainty

What is it about uncertainty that's threatening? Research shows that people with GAD hold several negative beliefs about uncertainty and its consequences, and that these beliefs or interpretations are what lead them to view unpredictable, novel, or ambiguous situations as negative and threatening (Birrell et al. 2011; Sexton and Dugas 2009). Specifically, there are three common negative beliefs about uncertainty.

BELIEF 1: IT'S UNFAIR TO HAVE TO FEEL UNCERTAIN

Most people with GAD view having to deal with the uncertainty in daily life as unfair and unacceptable. If you hold this belief, simply being in a state of uncertainty is upsetting to you. Some of our clients have said that they'd rather have bad news than not know what will happen because not knowing is more distressing.

This belief doesn't include any particular expectations about the outcome of unpredictable, novel, and ambiguous situations. Rather, these situations are viewed as negative simply due to the fact that they exist. People who view uncertainty in this manner tend to believe that others don't have to deal with as much uncertainty in their lives, or that capable and competent people experience more predictability and certainty in daily life.

BELIEF 2: UNCERTAIN EVENTS WILL TURN OUT VERY NEGATIVELY

Most people with GAD have an expectation that not only will unpredictable, novel, or ambiguous situations turn out badly, but that the negative outcome will be really terrible. For example, if they accidentally leave their phone at home, they might believe they'll miss a lot of important phone calls or texts, and that the people who tried to contact them will be very upset with them. If you hold this belief, it makes sense that you'd view any situation that carries some uncertainty as threatening.

As you can see, this belief includes two ideas: that novel, ambiguous, and unpredictable situations are highly likely to lead to negative events; and that the outcome will be extremely negative and overwhelming. So if you were to accidentally leave your phone at home, you would not only believe that you'll miss calls and texts (negative outcome), but that the missed messages will be important and the people who contacted you will be very angry (severe negative outcome).

BELIEF 3: I WON'T BE ABLE TO COPE WITH UNEXPECTED NEGATIVE OUTCOMES

Most people with GAD have the expectation that they won't be able to handle the negative outcomes that result from unpredictable, novel, or ambiguous situations. For example, if they get lost while driving somewhere new, they might believe it will take hours to find their way, or that they won't even know what to do.

If you hold this belief, you probably think that when you can't predict exactly what will happen in an unpredictable, novel, or ambiguous situation, you can't develop a plan ahead of time for dealing with unexpected negative outcomes (which is true). But then you also fear that not having a plan to cope with a negative situation means you will be completely overwhelmed or will deal with the situation very poorly if you're put on the spot. Worry therefore becomes a way of trying to plan for any situation where there's the potential for an unexpected negative outcome, in the hopes that this will allow you to avoid feeling overwhelmed or prevent you from coping with the situation poorly.

The Impact of Beliefs About Uncertainty

To see how beliefs about uncertainty can influence your reactions, let's go back to the example of being invited to a dance class. As you can see in figure 5.2, the beliefs that uncertainty is unfair, that it will lead to negative outcomes, and that it will prevent you from coping well are what lead to worry and anxiety.

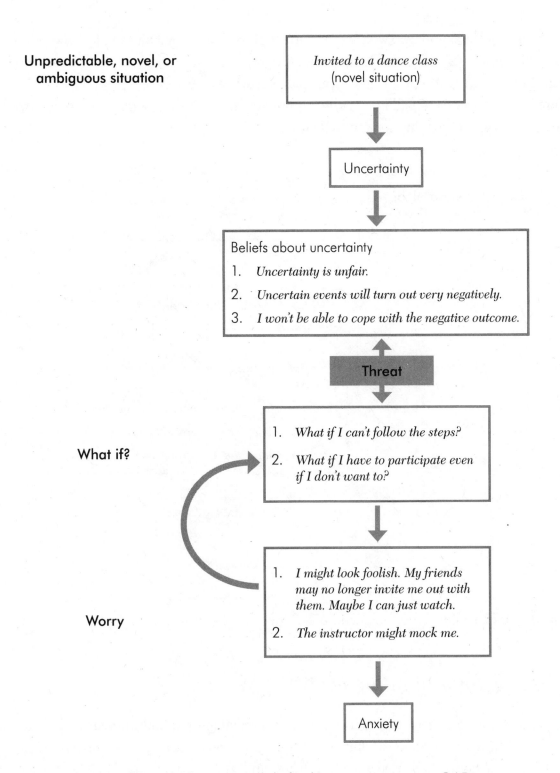

FIGURE 5.2. The influence of negative beliefs about uncertainty on GAD worry.

If, on the other hand, you were to view uncertainty as a normal part of life, believe that uncertain situations will probably turn out all right, and feel confident that you can cope even if they don't turn out all right, your reaction will be very different, as illustrated in figure 5.3. In this case, in addition to being unlikely to worry, you might even be excited about the prospect of trying something new.

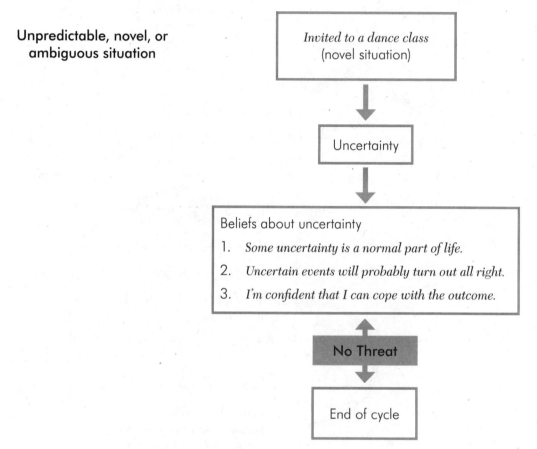

FIGURE 5.3. The influence of balanced beliefs about uncertainty.

Seeing Yourself in the Model of Worry

Because your reactions to uncertainty in novel, ambiguous, and unpredictable situations are fueling your worries, it's important to begin to recognize both the uncertain elements in situations that trigger your worries and the beliefs you hold about those situations.

You might have noticed that uncertainty is an abstract concept. When people are afraid of things such as flying, being in small spaces, or getting an injection, what they're threatened by is very clear and concrete. Being threatened by uncertainty has more to do with the nature of a situation, rather than the situation itself. An invitation to go to a dance class isn't naturally threatening; rather, the uncertainty in this novel situation makes it threatening. Therefore, it can be tricky to recognize when and where your intolerance of uncertainty is affecting your actions in daily life.

EXERCISE 5.1: In-Depth Worry Monitoring—Tracking Types of Triggers and Beliefs

In chapter 1, you completed the Worry Monitoring Log, which was designed to help you recognize your worries. Now that you have a better understanding of the situations that trigger your worries and the beliefs that make those situations threatening, you can start monitoring your worries at a deeper level. As a reminder, the more you understand your worries and anxiety, the better you'll be able to overcome them.

This monitoring form has two new columns compared to the version in exercise 1.3. In addition to recording triggers, worries, and anxiety level, you'll also keep track of the type of trigger and any negative beliefs about uncertainty that may have been involved in your reaction.

- **Type of trigger:** In this column, write down whether the triggering situation was unpredictable, novel, or ambiguous. Even if you're uncertain which one of these three types the situation falls into, do your best to pick one and write it down.

- **Negative beliefs about uncertainty:** In this column, write down any of the beliefs about uncertainty that may have played a role in your worry and anxiety about the situation. Did you find it unfair that you had to feel uncertain? Did you believe the situation would have a very negative outcome? Did you feel you'd be unable to cope with a potential negative outcome?

As with the Worry Monitoring Log in chapter 1, you don't need to fill out this form every time you have a worry. Instead, just fill it out three times a day for at least a week. With practice, you'll find that it gets easier to recognize your triggers, the type of trigger, and your negative beliefs about uncertainty in triggering situations. Here's an example of one day's worth of entries in the In-Depth Worry Monitoring Log.

SAMPLE IN-DEPTH WORRY MONITORING LOG

Situation or trigger	Type of trigger (unpredictable, novel, or ambiguous?)	Worry (what if?)	Negative beliefs about uncertainty (unfair, negative outcome, poor coping)	Anxiety (0 to 10)
A new instructor will be teaching my yoga class.	Unpredictable	What if I don't like him? What if the class is terrible? I might never find another class that I enjoy.	Unfair? Yes Negative outcome? Yes Poor coping? Yes	6
I sent a text to a friend and she didn't respond right away.	Ambiguous	What if I said something that upset her? What if she's mad at me?	Unfair? No Negative outcome? Yes Poor coping? No	3
I was transferred to a new department at work.	Novel	What if I can't figure out how to do my job in the new department? I might be overwhelmed or even lose my job.	Unfair? Yes Negative outcome? Yes Poor coping? Yes	8

Next, you'll find a blank form for your use. A downloadable version of this log is available at http://www.newharbinger.com/31519. You can also devise something similar in a small notebook or on an electronic device if you wish. We recommend filling it out for at least a week. In addition, keep these three tips from exercise 1.3 in mind when filling out the log:

1. Only complete the log three times a day.

2. Use your anxiety as a cue to reveal when you're worrying.

3. Write down your worries as soon as you can.

In-Depth Worry Monitoring Log

Situation or trigger	Type of trigger (unpredictable, novel, or ambiguous?)	Worry (what if?)	Negative beliefs about uncertainty (unfair, negative outcome, poor coping)	Anxiety (0 to 10)

Seeing Negative Beliefs About Uncertainty in a New Light

One of the benefits of recognizing the influence of negative beliefs about uncertainty on the worry cycle is that it provides you with a clear target in managing your worry. Specifically, it is by changing the way you interpret the uncertainty inherent in situations that you will ultimately reduce your overall worry. In practical terms, this means you don't need to learn how to manage each and every worry that comes to mind—just the beliefs about uncertainty that set off your worries in the first place. This is good news. Given that what you worry about can change from day to day, attempting to tackle each individual worry would be both time-consuming and mostly ineffective. Therefore, in the next three chapters, we'll set forth how you can change your interpretations of uncertainty in unpredictable, novel, and ambiguous situations, shifting your perception of uncertainty from something that's threatening to something that's normal, manageable, and sometimes even a desirable part of life.

CHAPTER 6

Intolerance of Uncertainty in Action: Identifying Safety Behaviors

I n chapter 5 you learned that the way in which you interpret ambiguous, novel, or unpredictable situations influences how you think and feel. In this chapter, you'll learn how your interpretations of uncertainty influence what you do. The focus of this chapter is on identifying and recognizing your *safety behaviors*—specific actions you take in an attempt to alleviate worry and anxiety.

Understanding Safety Behaviors

When you feel threatened, it's a natural human instinct to want to protect yourself. For example, if you're walking down a dark street at night and aren't feeling safe, you might start walking faster to get out of the area or look for well-lit places to walk where you might feel safer. This dynamic holds true for anxiety-provoking situations in daily life. When you worry about something bad happening, you're likely to do something to try to feel less anxious and prevent your feared outcome. These types of behaviors are called safety behaviors.

Unlike worries, which are typically experienced as uncontrollable, safety behaviors are deliberate actions you choose to do, and they're specific to the threat you encounter. For example, if you're afraid of being trapped in an elevator, your safety behavior might be having someone accompany you when you're on an elevator or avoiding elevators by taking the stairs.

The Function of Safety Behaviors

When you engage in a safety behavior, you're actually killing two birds with one stone: you're trying to avoid or eliminate a threatening situation, and you're also attempting to reduce your anxiety in that situation (Salkovskis, Clark, and Gelder 1996). Safety behaviors provide immediate results, with the goal being to feel better and avoid negative events in that very moment. For example, if you're invited to a party and you're worried that you won't know anyone and will therefore feel awkward, you might choose to simply not go to the party. This is one form of safety behavior. If you decide to avoid the party, you'll feel better right away and won't have to worry about the awkwardness of being at a social gathering and not knowing anyone there. However, if you decide that you really should go to the party, your safety behaviors might be to bring someone you know to the party and, once there, to only speak to that person and anyone else you already know. In this way, you're reducing both your anxiety and the likelihood that you'll feel awkward when talking to new people.

As you might have noticed from the two examples of safety behaviors just mentioned (avoiding the party, or going and only talking to people you know), there are two major types of safety behaviors (Salkovskis, Clark, and Gelder 1996). The first type is an avoidant (or escape) safety behavior. The goal of these actions is to avoid or delay the feared outcome. The benefit of this type of safety behavior is that you get an immediate decrease in anxiety and escape all aspects of the situation and its outcome, at least for the short term. The second type is an approach safety behavior. With approach behaviors, you enter an anxiety-provoking situation but do things to prevent or diminish feared consequences. For example, if you're afraid of getting lost while driving somewhere new for an appointment, you might drive to the location the day before or have someone accompany you to give you directions if you get lost. In this case, although you're driving to a new place, you're still avoiding the feared situation of getting lost and missing your appointment, and also reducing your anxiety, by practicing beforehand or driving with someone else in the car.

The Problem with Safety Behaviors

On the surface, it probably seems that safety behaviors are quite helpful. They can reduce anxiety in the moment and allow you to avoid, either directly or indirectly, negative outcomes from a threatening situation. Nevertheless, safety behaviors have a problematic effect on your initial fear: rather than reducing your fear of a particular situation, safety behaviors actually strengthen and maintain that fear. If you avoid going to a party, for example, you'll feel less anxious about that particular party, but your fear of going to social gatherings where you might not know anyone remains. You're just as afraid of the situation, and in fact, you might be more anxious the next time you're invited somewhere.

Another problem with safety behaviors is that they prevent you from finding out whether your fears are actually warranted in the situation. As discussed in chapter 2, thoughts are assumptions, so they may or may not be correct. However, if you act as if your thoughts are true, they'll feel true. Let's look at this using an example of having to give a presentation for work. Perhaps you're fearful that you won't do a good job and that your boss will be dissatisfied with your presentation. As a safety behavior, you might come up with an excuse for why you can't give the presentation that day and have a colleague do it instead. In this case, you'll feel as if you avoided giving a lousy talk that wouldn't have been well accepted. In other words, you're likely to think the negative outcome you predicted would have occurred had you not used that safety behavior.

The problem is, you can't know what would have happened. If you had actually given the presentation, you might not have done well. However, you might have given a great talk that would have impressed your boss, and perhaps you would have felt more confident giving presentations in the future. But because you acted as if you would have performed poorly, you're likely to believe that's exactly what would have happened. This keeps your fear of public speaking alive and strong.

Safety Behaviors in GAD

The actions you use to protect yourself in threatening situations are specific to the particular threat or fear. Different people may use different safety behaviors in the same situation depending on what they're afraid of in that situation. Let's say you're asked to take the elevator to the top of a ten-story building. If you're afraid of being stuck in the elevator, your safety behavior might be to take the stairs. If instead you're afraid of heights, you might take the elevator but avoid looking out the windows when you reach the top floor.

In GAD, because the theme of threat is uncertainty, your safety behaviors will specifically target the uncertainty in unpredictable, novel, and ambiguous situations. The goal of GAD safety behaviors is to avoid, eliminate, reduce, or otherwise get around the uncertain aspects of a situation. And because uncertainty can be present in so many situations, there are many different types of safety behaviors people with GAD use.

GAD Safety Behaviors: Approach Strategies

The approach strategies people with GAD use when entering unpredictable, novel, or ambiguous situations vary widely, but all are designed to minimize or eliminate as much uncertainty as possible. The primary categories are discussed in the following sections. Of course, the specific form these behaviors take depends on the individual and the situation.

Excessive Reassurance Seeking

People with GAD often ask for reassurance from friends and family for a variety of reasons. If this is a safety behavior you use, you might find that you often ask others about decisions or choices you have to make, and that you do so numerous times. Examples include repeatedly asking several people whether you should buy something (a car, a new pair of jeans, or new shoes) or asking what others think of a decision you're considering (going to see a movie or choosing where and when to go on vacation). Everyone asks for others' opinions sometimes. It becomes a safety behavior if you typically feel anxious about following through on an action or decision without repeatedly asking others whether they think it's a good idea.

Double-Checking

Double-checking involves repeatedly going over things you're working on to make sure they're correct. For example, you might double-check an e-mail or a text you wrote by rereading it several times, or perhaps you review messages you've sent to reduce the uncertainty that you might have written something incorrectly or expressed yourself poorly. Perhaps you excessively reread papers or reports you've written to make sure there are no mistakes.

Many people with GAD also check on loved ones repeatedly. Do you ever call or text friends or family members several times if they're late or away from home? If you do, this is probably a safety behavior you're using to reduce uncertainty in an ambiguous situation: because you aren't 100 percent sure your loved ones are safe, you're trying to eliminate your uncertainty by checking.

Excessive Information Seeking

Another safety behavior in the approach category involves looking up information (these days, usually on the Internet) when you're unsure about something or when making a decision. For people with GAD, looking up information can become a lengthy process. You also might find that you look up information when you're unsure about even small decisions or actions. For example, before making a purchase you might look up an item at several online stores, and then go to multiple stores in person to compare prices and quality. Other possibilities include reading all of the reviews you can find on different hotels before booking a room, or going online to look up medical information when you notice a small physical change, such as a mole or a bump on your skin, and you aren't sure what it is. All of these actions are designed to increase your certainty in unpredictable, novel, or ambiguous situations. And again, although most people do these types of things on occasion, if you're spending a great deal of time trying to obtain as much information as possible before making a decision, this is probably a safety behavior.

Excessive List Making

Many people with GAD see themselves as world-class champions of list making. They might spend up to an hour every day developing new lists for the day, and may develop sublists within the primary list (things to do at home, things to do at work, things to do in the future, and so on). This is probably an approach safety behavior if you do it in an effort to reduce your uncertainty about what to do over the course of your day and to make 100 percent sure that you don't forget anything you might need to do.

Doing Everything Yourself

A common safety behavior is refusing to delegate tasks to others. When you do everything yourself, you can be 100 percent sure that tasks are being done, and that they're being done in the way that you want them done. You might find that you prefer to take care of all the household duties like doing laundry, making beds, and washing the dishes so you know they're done correctly, or you might do everything yourself at work. However, as is the case with most every safety behavior, not allowing anyone else to help with tasks can become very time-consuming and stressful. Reducing or eliminating uncertainty can easily start to feel like a full-time job in itself.

Doing Things for Others

In addition to refusing to delegate tasks, many people with GAD also try to do things for others. If you have children, you might find that you hover over them while they're doing their homework, pack their sports gear before a game to make sure that they don't forget anything, and drive them everywhere so you don't have to cope with the uncertainty of whether they'll arrive somewhere safely on their own. With other family members and friends, you might volunteer to prepare all of the food for a family dinner or take care of all household finances to ensure that everything is done correctly and on time. Unfortunately, this type of overprotection often feels like nagging to others, particularly to children.

GAD Safety Behaviors: Avoidance Strategies

The approach behaviors just described involve entering into unpredictable, novel, or ambiguous situations with strategies aimed at reducing the uncertainty within a given situation. In contrast, avoidance strategies involve eliminating uncertainty by steering clear of these situations altogether, or at least delaying entering them as long as possible.

Avoidance

An obvious form of avoidance behavior is avoidance, pure and simple. Avoidance allows you to bypass the uncertainty of an unpredictable, novel, or ambiguous situation by simply not placing yourself in the situation. The forms this takes are endless. You might cancel a meeting with your accountant because you don't know whether you'll have enough money to pay your taxes. If you're invited to go to a new restaurant, you might decide not to go because you aren't sure whether you'll like the food. Or you might avoid taking an exercise class at your gym if you aren't familiar with the instructor.

Another form of avoidance involves deferring decision making to others in unpredictable, novel, and ambiguous situations. For example, if you're getting together with friends, you might ask them to decide what activity everyone will do, allowing you to avoid the uncertainty of choosing an activity others may not enjoy.

Procrastination

Procrastination is a common form of avoidant safety behavior. It offers the benefit of simply putting things off until a later date, rather than technically avoiding anything. For example, perhaps you've procrastinated in making an appointment to see your doctor after noticing a nonspecific symptom, such as a mole or a lingering ache in your chest, because of the uncertain outcome of medical results in this kind of ambiguous situation.

Procrastination can also be a strategic safety behavior used to delay the amount of time available to worry about decisions you make or how you perform on a task. Some people find that if they delay completing a task until the very last minute, once it's completed there's very little time available to worry about it.

A major problem with procrastination is that it comes at a high cost. If you consistently delay entering into situations that are unpredictable, novel, or ambiguous, you might miss out on opportunities, others might get upset with you, or over time a small problem you avoided can become a big problem.

Partial Commitment

Another avoidant safety behavior is a tendency to only partially commit to people, situations, or plans. For example, you might keep friends or romantic partners at a distance, largely because relationships are unpredictable situations where there's no guarantee about the long-term outcome. You also might not fully commit to plans, perhaps including not consistently following through on the exercises in this workbook. The act of keeping one foot out the door is strategic because as long as you aren't fully invested in something, you can step away quickly if it doesn't appear to be working out or if the uncertain nature of the situation feels overwhelming. However, this strategy has drawbacks. For example, you're likely to feel isolated from others if you keep them at a distance. And although partially investing in things can shield you from negative consequences, it also prevents you from fully enjoying any positive consequences.

Impulsive Decision Making

Many decisions in life aren't clear-cut. For example, if you want to plant flowers in your garden, what are the best flowers? What's the right program to sign up for in college? What's the best movie to see this weekend? These types of situations are ambiguous because there's no right answer. Different people will have different answers, and there's no way to be certain what will be best for you until you've made a choice and given it a try. Some people with GAD use impulsive decision making as a safety behavior when they face ambiguous choices.

If this is safety behavior you use, you might make choices quickly and randomly, similar to flipping a coin or rolling dice to make a decision. Once you've decided, even though you enter the chosen situation, you've avoided the responsibility for the outcome because your decision wasn't well thought out. For example, if you have to choose what restaurant to go to one evening, you might wait until the last minute and then pick the closest place that will still take a reservation. If you're dissatisfied with the choice, you likely feel less connected to the outcome because you didn't own your decision. But on the flip side, you don't get to own successes when you don't put real thought into a decision.

Aren't Many of These Behaviors Normal?

Many of our clients have observed that most people regularly engage in all of these GAD safety behaviors. Indeed, this is true. Most everyone makes to-do lists, looks up information online, double-checks e-mails or other written work, procrastinates, avoids certain things, and so on. In fact, many of these behaviors can be viewed positively. For example, if you're afraid of being in enclosed spaces, you might take the stairs instead of the elevator and ride your bike rather than take the bus. Both of these behaviors are actually recommended, healthy activities, so how can they be negative?

The reason lies in what motivates the safety behavior. With safety behaviors, the problem isn't so much what you do but why you do it. Think of it as the difference between doing things based on choice versus doing things because of anxiety. When you choose to do something, it's a preference. For example, you might prefer to do the dishes and make the bed first thing in the morning so everything is tidy when you come home. However, if you're running late one morning, you'd probably feel okay about skipping these activities; although you prefer to do them, you can also choose not to do them when circumstances dictate otherwise. On the other hand, the reason you do the dishes and make the bed each morning might be rooted in anxiety, perhaps due to worry that if someone were to come over unexpectedly your home wouldn't look neat and tidy. In this case, if you're running late one morning and don't have the time to do these household chores, you'd probably become very anxious and either stay to do them anyway or leave home distracted and anxious. You might even come home early to attend to these chores.

Although the behaviors are the same in both cases (doing the dishes, making the bed), the motivation behind the actions is very different. When you do something out of anxiety, you aren't really choosing to do it; rather, you feel compelled to do it. From a CBT perspective, it's worth working on behaviors that are driven by anxiety. Then, if you later decide to continue doing these things, you're doing them because you truly want to, not because you feel you have to.

EXERCISE 6.1: Identifying Your Safety Behaviors

Now that you know the most common types of safety behaviors used by people with GAD, you can begin to identify your own. Use the In-Depth Worry Monitoring Log from exercise 5.1 to help you identify some of the safety behaviors you engage in to cope with your worries. Then continue monitoring your safety behaviors for the next week or two. As with the worry monitoring forms, aim to make about three entries per day, recording them as soon as possible after the event that triggered your safety behavior. Use feelings of anxiety as a cue to help you notice which situations make you uncomfortable, and then tune in to how you try to reduce the anxiety and deal with the situation.

We've provided a blank form you can use for this (also available for download at http://www.newharbinger.com/31519). But first, here's an example to help you see how it works.

SAMPLE SAFETY BEHAVIORS MONITORING FORM

Situation	Worry (what if?)	Safety behavior (what you did)
A new instructor will be teaching my yoga class.	What if I don't like him? What if the class is terrible? I might never find another class that I enjoy.	I avoided going to the class. (avoidance)
I sent a text to a friend and she didn't respond right away.	What if I said something that upset her? What if she's mad at me?	I reread all of our texts to see what I had written. (double-checking) I texted some other friends to ask for advice about what to do. (reassurance seeking)
I was transferred to a new department at work.	What if I can't figure out how to do my job in the new department? I might be overwhelmed or even lose my job.	I spent hours looking up information online about the new department and the people who work there. (information seeking)

SAFETY BEHAVIORS MONITORING FORM

Situation	Worry (what if?)	Safety behavior (what you did)

Next, go through the list of GAD safety behaviors and, in the worksheet that follows, write down which strategies you use to cope with your worries. We highly recommend recording a personal example of a situation where you used a particular strategy. Knowing the safety behaviors you commonly use in your daily life will be helpful in the next chapter, when you start tackling these behaviors.

IDENTIFYING YOUR SAFETY BEHAVIORS

Excessive reassurance seeking (repeatedly asking others for advice or for reassurance about decisions you've made)

Do you use this strategy?   Yes _____   No _____

Personal example: _____

_____

_____

Double-checking (going over written work, e-mails, or texts to make sure there are no mistakes; checking up on family and friends whenever you're unsure about where they are or whether they're okay)

Do you use this strategy?   Yes _____   No _____

Personal example: _____

_____

_____

Excessive information seeking (going to multiple sources to get information before making a decision in order to be sure about what to do; looking up information excessively, usually online, about purchases, medical issues, directions, and so on)

Do you use this strategy?   Yes _____   No _____

Personal example: _____

_____

_____

Excessive list making (making multiple to-do lists, usually every day, and often for an extended period of time)

Do you use this strategy?　　　Yes _____　　　No _____

Personal example: _____

_____

_____

Doing everything yourself (doing all tasks rather than delegating some to others, usually in an attempt to ensure that things are done when and how you prefer)

Do you use this strategy?　　　Yes _____　　　No _____

Personal example: _____

_____

_____

Doing things for others (not allowing others to do things for themselves, including doing tasks for children even when the task is age-appropriate)

Do you use this strategy?　　　Yes _____　　　No _____

Personal example: _____

_____

_____

Avoidance (avoiding situations, activities, or people that are unpredictable, novel, or ambiguous; avoiding responsibility for decision making by asking others to make choices or decisions for you)

Do you use this strategy?   Yes _____   No _____

Personal example: _____

_____

_____

Procrastination (delaying decisions or tasks that are unpredictable, novel, or ambiguous; deliberately delaying a task or decision until the last moment in order to reduce the amount of time available to worry about the finished task or chosen decision)

Do you use this strategy?   Yes _____   No _____

Personal example: _____

_____

_____

Partial commitment (avoiding fully committing to relationships, activities, or decisions in order to minimize exposure to potential negative outcomes)

Do you use this strategy?   Yes _____   No _____

Personal example: _____

_____

_____

Impulsive decision making (deliberately making a quick and random decision in an attempt to reduce responsibility and negative emotions if the outcome is negative)

Do you use this strategy?   Yes _____   No _____

Personal example: _____

_____

_____

Taking on Safety Behaviors

Over the last two chapters, you've learned how negative beliefs about uncertainty lead to worry by causing you to interpret unpredictable, novel, and ambiguous situations as threatening, and you've learned that they also influence your behavior. Unfortunately, although safety behaviors are an attempt to cope with worry, they inadvertently maintain the cycle of worry over the long term. This is because safety behaviors prevent you from finding out whether the outcomes of uncertain situations would in fact be very negative and whether you could in fact cope with any difficulties that might arise. With this in mind, the next chapter discusses how to challenge your beliefs about uncertainty directly by testing out what actually happens when you refrain from engaging in the safety behaviors you use in daily life.

CHAPTER 7

Tolerating Uncertainty: Testing Out Beliefs About Uncertainty

Over the past two chapters, we discussed how negative beliefs about the uncertainty in situations in daily life can influence how you think (leading to worry) and feel (creating anxiety), as well as what you do (engaging in safety behaviors). You now know that changing your negative beliefs about uncertainty will have significant positive effects: you'll be less likely to view unpredictable, novel, and ambiguous situations as threatening, which will help you worry less, be less anxious, and engage in fewer time-consuming safety behaviors. Given that thinking differently about the uncertainty in day-to-day situations can have such beneficial effects, the next logical question is: How do you change a belief?

Changing the Way You Think

Changing what you believe or how you think can be quite tricky. Many of our clients come to CBT with the assumption that their thinking will be "reprogrammed" or that they'll learn to "think positively." This isn't the case. You change the way you think about something in the same way you might get others to change their mind on an issue: you make a compelling case that they can truly believe. For example, say you have a friend who lives in the city, and you want her to believe that living in the country is a better choice for her. You won't change her mind just by asking her to change it. You might tell her about the benefits of living in the country: the peace and quiet, the slower pace of life, and the clean air. You might also tell her that living in the city is more expensive, that it's noisy, and there's more pollution; or you might encourage her to take a vacation in the country to experience what it's like. If your arguments and the evidence you gather are compelling, your friend might change her belief about the value of living in the country.

We use this same approach for changing beliefs about uncertainty in day-to-day situations. If you want to think differently about uncertainty, you can't simply tell yourself to do so. Rather, you'll need to gather evidence that will allow you to see whether your current beliefs about uncertainty provide an accurate representation of situations that lead to worry.

One of the best ways to gather evidence for or against a belief is through actual experience. For example, if you avoid going to the dentist because you think it will be very painful, a good way to find out whether your belief is accurate is to actually go to the dentist. By doing so, you'll be in a good position to determine whether dental work is as painful as you'd expected. In this way, by changing your behavior, you put yourself in a position to obtain factual information about the situation. This information might lead you to change your belief.

With this in mind, you can also obtain evidence for or against your beliefs about uncertainty in unpredictable, novel, and ambiguous situations by changing your behavior. Specifically, by decreasing your safety behaviors, you can find out whether uncertainty is as negative and threatening as you think it is.

Behavioral Experiments

When we introduced safety behaviors, we mentioned that one of the major problems with avoiding something you're afraid of is that you never get to find out whether there's any reason to fear it. For example, if you think planes are very unsafe and likely to crash, you might avoid flying. However, if you never get on a plane or never even go near airports, how will you ever know whether air travel is actually safe? Because you never get to find out for yourself if your fears and beliefs are accurate, you're likely to keep holding on to them and will therefore continue avoiding air travel and going to airports.

However, by changing your behavior, in this case perhaps going to an airport to watch planes arrive and depart or even taking a short flight yourself, you can begin to gather evidence about whether air travel is as dangerous as you think. In CBT, this is called a *behavioral experiment*. Behavioral experiments allow you to directly test beliefs by predicting what you think will happen in a feared situation, deliberately entering into that situation, and then finding out what really happens.

Let's say you think you're socially awkward and don't know how to make conversation with others. If you believe this, you might avoid talking to anyone, including salespeople and cashiers, or you might keep any conversation to a minimum—for example, giving mostly yes or no answers. In this case, your behavior is preventing you from finding out whether you would in fact be able to have a conversation with someone. For this fear, a behavioral experiment could involve choosing to make small talk with the cashier at a local coffee shop. You might predict that the person won't want to talk to you or will act as if you're weird or odd when speaking to you, maybe by rolling his eyes. By deliberately engaging in this experiment, you can find out what actually happens and determine whether your prediction, and therefore your belief, was accurate.

Behavioral Experiments in GAD

For people with GAD, safety behaviors revolve around reducing, avoiding, or eliminating uncertainty. However, these behaviors prevent you from finding out whether engaging in them is in fact necessary, and whether your beliefs about uncertainty are accurate. For example, if you avoid driving a new route because you're worried that you'll get lost, a safety behavior of avoidance successfully eliminates the uncertainty of this unpredictable situation. When you choose not to drive, you no longer have to deal with the uncertainty of navigating an unfamiliar route. In this case, you'd probably believe you avoided the negative outcome of getting lost, as well as feelings of being overwhelmed and unable to cope once you got lost. Both of these feared predictions can be directly tested using a behavioral experiment.

To conduct a behavioral experiment around this worry, you might decide to drive to a location that's within your neighborhood but that you've never been to before. In this case, your predicted outcome might be that you'll get lost and won't be able to find your way again. Your experiment would allow you to directly test out at least one, and potentially two or three negative beliefs about uncertainty:

- **Did the uncertain element in this situation lead to a negative outcome?** In this example, do you actually get lost when you drive somewhere unfamiliar?

- **If a negative outcome occurred, how bad was it?** If you get lost, is it disastrous or catastrophic?

- **If a negative outcome occurred, how did you cope?** Were you eventually able to find your way? Was it an overwhelmingly difficult situation to manage?

Because GAD behavioral experiments are designed to allow you to investigate both the outcome of situations where there's uncertainty and your ability to cope with negative outcomes should they occur, you can obtain information about your beliefs regardless of whether the outcome is positive or negative. If the outcome is positive, your behavioral experiment might play out as follows.

Experiment: *I'll drive to a bookstore in my neighborhood that I've never driven to before.*

Predicted outcome: *I'll get lost on my way to the store. It will take long time for me to find my way, if I can do it at all.*

Actual outcome: *I found my way to the bookstore without getting lost.*

Coping: *No coping was necessary.*

This behavioral experiment allows you to test out the belief that the uncertain element in the situation will lead to a negative outcome. In the preceding example, the findings from the experiment reveal that the prediction was incorrect. And because the outcome was positive (you didn't get lost), you didn't need to cope with the predicted negative outcome.

Now let's suppose that the outcome wasn't positive.

Experiment: *I'll drive to a bookstore in my neighborhood that I've never driven to before.*

Predicted outcome: *I'll get lost on my way to the store. It will take long time for me to find my way, if I can do it at all.*

Actual outcome: *I did get lost. I got confused about the cross street just before the bookstore.*

Coping: *I stopped the car and asked for directions. I was only one block away. I eventually found the store.*

The results of this experiment can now allow you to test out all three beliefs:

- **Did the uncertain element in this situation lead to a negative outcome?** *Yes and no. I predicted I would get lost, and I actually did. However, I also predicted that it would take a long time for me to find my way, but I found my way quickly after I asked for directions.*

- **If a negative outcome occurred, how bad was it?** *It actually wasn't that bad. After asking for directions, it only took a few minutes for me to find the store.*

- **If a negative outcome occurred, how did you cope?** *Overall, I think I coped pretty well. Although I was flustered when I got lost, I think it was a good idea to stop and ask for directions. I didn't get overwhelmed by the situation.*

A key aspect of behavioral experiments is that you don't know what will actually happen. In the preceding example, if you test out your belief by driving somewhere new, you could be right and end up very lost, or you could be wrong or partially wrong (getting lost but then finding your way again easily). In this way, conducting behavioral experiments can help you change your thinking about situations through direct experience. If an experiment shows that your prediction was wrong, you might start to adopt different beliefs (for example, that you are, in fact, able to navigate unfamiliar places). If you believe this, you'll probably stop avoiding driving to new places and will experience little to no anxiety when you do. If, on the other hand, your prediction was entirely accurate (you got very lost and couldn't find your way again for hours), your behavior will likely remain unchanged. However, in this case the experiment would still be worthwhile, because it would allow you to develop a plan for coping with future situations where you might need to drive somewhere new.

In short, behavioral experiments allow you to obtain *objective* evidence about a situation so you don't have to rely on what you think might happen. So if your thoughts about a situation cause you a great deal of anxiety or lead you to engage in behaviors that reduce your quality of life, it's a good idea to test out whether those thoughts are actually correct.

Developing Your Own Behavioral Experiments

In order to begin setting up your own behavioral experiments, you need to identify some of your safety behaviors that could be tested. Your first experiments should be small, and they should have a clear, observable outcome. For example, if you tend to frequently check your phone for texts or messages out of fear that you might miss something important, you might decide to not check your phone for an hour or two.

Experiment: *I won't check my cell phone for two hours.*

Predicted outcome: *I'll miss an important call or text.*

This is a good first experiment because you can choose how long the experiment will be (thirty minutes, one hour, two hours, all day), and at the end you'll have a clear outcome: When you finally do check your phone, you'll see whether you missed any important messages and whether the outcome is truly negative or catastrophic. Here are a few other good initial experiments:

- Going to a new restaurant or movie without reading a review

- Ordering a meal that you've never tried before

- Making a small purchase with little to no research beforehand

- Making a small decision without asking for reassurance from others

- Calling a friend you've lost touch with

- Going to the grocery store without a list

- Delegating a small task to a coworker

- Delegating a household chore to a family member

- Making plans for yourself and some friends (if you tend to avoid making plans for others)

- Letting someone else make plans without consulting you beforehand (if you're someone who tends to want to do everything yourself)

Tips for Conducting Behavioral Experiments

Behavioral experiments can sometimes be challenging to set up, especially when you're new to them. Here are some tips on how to conduct them.

START SMALL

Whenever you're deliberately choosing to do something that leads to anxiety, it's a good idea to start with things that are relatively easy. For example, if you're afraid of dogs, you might start by looking at a picture of a dog or being near a small puppy. The initial experiments you do should cause only mild to moderate anxiety. To determine this, you can use the same scale as in earlier exercises, rating your fear when trying an experiment on a scale from 0 to 10. Aim for something that doesn't cause more anxiety than a 4 or 5 out of 10. That way the experiment will be challenging but doable. It's better to take a small successful step than to try to take a huge step and fail. As you get more confident, you'll soon be able to try more challenging experiments.

With this in mind, it's also important to start small in terms of the number of behavioral experiments you conduct. Some of our clients are understandably excited at the notion of testing out the accuracy of their negative beliefs about uncertainty and want to start by conducting a different experiment every day for a week. Although this kind of motivation is excellent, deliberately facing the uncertainty in day-to-day situations can be more difficult than expected, especially if you've spent most of your life trying to avoid uncertainty. If you plan to do too many experiments and are unable to complete them all, for example planning to do seven over the course of a week and only accomplishing four, you're likely to feel discouraged. However, if you plan to do three experiments over the course of a week and complete four, you'll probably be quite proud of yourself and feel motivated to try more experiments the following week. So start small and give yourself a chance to succeed, then increase the number of behavioral experiments you set for yourself.

EXPECT TO BE ANXIOUS

When you conduct a behavioral experiment, you're deliberately doing something you've avoided in the past. Because of this, it is not only normal to feel anxious when you do them, it's actually expected. We often tell our clients that if they tried an experiment and had no anxiety at all while doing it, they might have accidentally cheated. For example, let's say that you decided to let your children pack their own bags when staying overnight at a friend's place. (This is a great experiment if you worry that your kids will forget something, in which case your safety behavior is likely to be doing everything for them.) However, if you watch them pack their bags or remind them of all the things they might need before they pack, you're undermining the experiment. Because of your approach, you probably won't feel anxious, so you won't learn much from the experiment. In short, if you feel anxious when you're doing a behavioral experiment, you're on the right track.

REPEAT AN EXPERIMENT MORE THAN ONCE

Keep in mind that behavioral experiments are designed to test the accuracy of your negative beliefs about uncertainty in unpredictable, novel, and ambiguous situations. So as with any good experiment, you may need to repeat some of your experiments several times before you can make realistic conclusions about the outcome. For example, suppose you decide to go to the grocery store without a list to test out the prediction that you'll forget something at the store. Perhaps the actual outcome is that you don't forget anything. If you're like most people, you'll probably put that down to luck. So even if the outcome is positive, you're unlikely to change your beliefs because you only tried the experiment once. If, however, you try the same experiment multiple times and the outcome is always positive, or if you consistently find that you're able to cope well even when the outcome is negative, your beliefs about the threat of uncertainty in that situation will probably start to change.

EXERCISE 7.1: Testing Out Negative Beliefs About Uncertainty

As a first exercise in testing out your negative beliefs about uncertainty, we recommend that you conduct approximately three behavioral experiments a week. As your confidence in conducting behavioral experiments grows, you can choose to complete a greater number of weekly exercises. You can use your Safety Behavior Monitoring Form from exercise 6.1 to help you identify safety behaviors you might choose to let go of in behavioral experiments. As noted earlier, it's important to record your experiences when doing the exercises in this book. This will allow you to see any patterns and arrive at a conclusion based on your actual experience.

As you begin to conduct behavioral experiments, use the following form to record the results. A version of the form with additional space is also available for download at http://www.newharbinger.com/31519, and we encourage you to print additional copies so you can record the results of all of your experiments. This information will help you track your progress. It will also come in handy in later exercises.

Here are some pointers on what to record in each column of the form:

- **Experiment:** Before conducting the experiment, write down what you'll do in the first column. Make sure the experiment involves deliberately entering into an unpredictable, novel, or ambiguous situation without engaging in a behavior that might reduce or eliminate the uncertainty of the situation.

- **Predicted outcome:** Also before conducting the experiment, record what you fear could happen in the second column.

- **Actual outcome:** After you've completed your experiment, record what actually happened in the third column. To aid in tracking your results, in addition to describing the outcome, you can also indicate whether it was positive, negative, or neutral.

- **Coping:** If the actual outcome was negative in some way, use the fourth column to describe how you coped with the situation. What did you do when things didn't go well?

RESULTS OF BEHAVIORAL EXPERIMENTS

Experiment	Predicted outcome	Actual outcome	Coping
I won't check my cell phone for two hours.	I'll miss an important call or text, and the person will be angry.	No one called or texted.	No coping necessary.
I won't check my cell phone for two hours.	I'll miss an important call or text, and the person will be angry.	My friend texted me to change our plans for tonight.	Contacted my friend to confirm change of plans. She didn't mention the missed text.

Troubleshooting Behavioral Experiments

One of the advantages of working with a CBT therapist is that a therapist can guide you in setting up behavioral experiments and troubleshooting experiments that don't seem to be working well. If, however, you're doing this work on your own, we can provide some guidance on a few specific difficulties that some of our clients have experienced.

Difficulty Coming Up with Experiments

It isn't uncommon for people to struggle initially with identifying experiments to test out their negative beliefs. This can happen because even though you're probably engaging in numerous safety behaviors every day, they've become so woven into your daily life that it's challenging to even notice yourself doing them. If the first experiments we listed earlier in this chapter don't seem appropriate to you, spend another week completing the Safety Behaviors Monitoring Form in exercise 6.1, taking the time to really notice your thoughts, feelings, and behaviors each time you make an entry. Use your feelings of anxiety as a cue to help you notice which situations make you uncomfortable and how you try to reduce the anxiety and deal with the situation. Once you find a safety behavior that you engage in, remember that it doesn't matter how small your first behavioral experiments are. Also, don't feel you have to come up with a wide variety of experiments right away; you can—and should—do most experiments several times, if possible.

Not Experiencing Any Anxiety

You might find that you purposely didn't engage in a safety behavior and, to your surprise, didn't experience any anxiety. This can occur if you inadvertently replace one safety behavior with another. If this is happening, you may need to adjust your behavioral experiment. For example, suppose your experiment is to buy a new pair of jeans without first doing excessive research or seeking reassurance; your plan is to go into the store and buy the first pair of jeans you see. Although this might seem like an excellent experiment (and for some people it is), if you don't experience any anxiety, your experiment might involve an unintended safety behavior. Buying the first pair of jeans you see could be an impulsive decision (like flipping a coin) that doesn't cause anxiety because you didn't bear any responsibility for the choice. In these types of situations, aim for the middle ground. For this particular experiment, that might mean trying on two or three different styles of jeans and then picking one without seeking reassurance from others.

This type of problem can also occur if you're conducting an experiment in which you delegate a task to someone. Let's say you typically take charge of all major projects at work, and as an experiment, you decide to give one project to a colleague rather than coordinate it yourself. Again, this might be an excellent experiment for some people. However, if you don't experience any anxiety when you do it, it may be that when you handed over the project, you completely washed your hands of it and absolved yourself of any responsibility. A good middle ground for this experiment would be to delegate the project to your colleague and then periodically check in to see how she's doing with it—without giving suggestions or advice about how she should handle the project.

Not Being Motivated to Do Behavioral Experiments

Because behavioral experiments lead to feelings of anxiety, it's absolutely normal to be somewhat reluctant to try them. Many of our clients have reported that they weren't motivated to follow through on experiments for this very reason. But though this is perfectly understandable, waiting until you feel motivated before starting something isn't an effective approach. Contrary to common opinion, motivation doesn't precede action; it follows action. Only after you do something, even if you don't feel like doing it, can you start to feel motivated. For example, you might not feel motivated to go to the gym, but if you make yourself go, you'll probably be proud of yourself afterward, motivating you to go again.

If you're having a hard time getting started on behavioral experiments due to low motivation, schedule a specific time and date to try one, for example, "On Wednesday evening, I'll try out the Thai restaurant in my neighborhood that I've never been to." Then follow through, whether or not you feel motivated at the time. Sticking with your initial experiments may feel challenging, but once you gain some momentum, you'll find yourself increasingly motivated to keep moving forward.

Not Being Able to Follow Through Without Using Safety Behaviors

If you attempt an experiment several times but feel too anxious to follow through without using some sort of safety behavior, you're probably trying an experiment that's too difficult at present. Remember, it's best to start small, even if it feels like such a small step won't make much of a difference in your life. Some of our clients tell us that they want to start with challenging experiments in order to see improvements in their worry and anxiety as quickly as possible. This is also absolutely understandable. But again, it's better to take small successful steps than to take too big a step and fail. When you use the strategies in this workbook, where you start isn't where you'll finish. Although you might begin with small experiments, you'll move on to bigger and more challenging experiments as time goes on. Be patient with yourself and aim for success, no matter how small your first steps are.

EXERCISE 7.2: Reviewing Your Findings

We recommend that you continue to engage in behavioral experiments to test your negative beliefs about uncertainty for several weeks. Then you can begin to draw some conclusions about the results. At the end of each week, have an experiment review session with yourself, sitting down with your completed Results of Behavioral Experiments worksheets and assessing your findings to date. Ask yourself the following questions when reviewing your experiments and record your answers either in the following form (available for download at http://www.newharbinger.com/31519), or on paper or electronically.

Reviewing Your Behavioral Experiments

1. How often was the actual outcome the same as the predicted outcome? _____

   _____

   Review the actual outcome in each of your behavioral experiments, then answer the following questions:

2. How often was the outcome positive? _____

3. How often was the outcome neutral? _____

4. How often was the outcome negative? _____

   For those cases in which the actual outcome was negative, answer the following questions:

5. Was it as bad as you expected? Describe how bad it was:

   _____

   _____

6. Do you think you handled the negative outcome well? Describe how you handled it:

   _____

   _____

7. Was it very difficult to deal with? Describe how you felt:

   _____

   _____

8. If you'd had the time to worry about it beforehand, do you think you would have handled the situation better? Describe how this might have affected the outcome:

_____

_____

9. Looking at your answers to these questions, what are some of your initial conclusions? What can you say about the accuracy of your beliefs?

_____

_____

_____

Strengthening Your Tolerance of Uncertainty

Because beliefs about uncertainty are fuel for the engine of worry, it's important to give yourself lots of time to practice the kinds of behavioral experiments described in this chapter. You can only change your mind about something when you have compelling evidence for doing so. In the case of behavioral experiments, the overarching goal is to obtain enough evidence to determine whether uncertainty in unpredictable, novel, and ambiguous situations leads to a high rate of negative outcomes. And in those cases where the experiment does lead to a negative outcome, the purpose is to determine whether those outcomes have severe or catastrophic consequences and whether you're able to handle negative outcomes without feeling overwhelmed. The more often you do behavioral experiments, the more likely you are to have confidence in what you learn. As much as possible, try to find opportunities in your daily life to test the accuracy of your beliefs about uncertainty. In our experience, the best behavioral experiments are those people come up with themselves when they recognize an opportunity to truly discover what happens when they deliberately invite uncertainty into their lives. The next chapter will help you move further in this direction.

CHAPTER 8

Moving Toward
Embracing Uncertainty

B y now you should have some experience with what happens when you invite uncertainty into your life. Hopefully the behavioral experiments you've conducted have allowed you to see that the uncertainty in unpredictable, novel, and ambiguous situations isn't as threatening as you originally believed. Even if you're now on board with this idea, the content of this chapter might surprise you. We're going to invite you to consider that not only is it tolerable to allow some uncertainty into your life, it might actually be desirable. With that in mind, this chapter will help you widen the scope of your behavioral experiments and begin to embrace uncertainties in daily life.

Widening the Scope of Behavioral Experiments

Before we discuss how facing uncertainty might actually be beneficial on occasion, we'd like you to get some broader experience with the effects of inviting uncertainty into the many facets of your daily life. The following sections will describe different ways to broaden the scope of your behavioral experiments so that you'll feel more confident that the results of your experiments can be generalized to almost any circumstance in your life.

Diversifying Your Behavioral Experiments

Uncertainty can be present in most any situation in your life—at work or at school, at home, in your social life, and more. Therefore, in order to most effectively gather information regarding the accuracy of your beliefs about unpredictable, novel, and ambiguous situations, it's best to conduct behavioral experiments across all the domains of your life. This will give you a broad idea about the outcome of uncertain situations in your daily life, and also help you assess your general ability to cope with negative outcomes no matter what the situation.

In practical terms, this means extending your behavioral experiments into different areas of your life. For example, suppose that all of your experiments thus far have involved facing uncertainty in work-related situations, such as delegating work tasks, volunteering for new projects, or making decisions without asking for reassurance from others. These are all excellent experiments. The next step is to try experiments in different environments. In this case, you might make decisions that involve you or your family at home, such as deciding what to make for dinner without asking for reassurance, or allowing your children to do the dishes without supervising them. Or you might begin to incorporate tests related to your social life, such as trying a new activity or buying tickets to a show without researching it beforehand. The next exercise will help you begin to branch out.

EXERCISE 8.1: Doing Behavioral Experiments in Other Areas of Life

Take a moment to review the experiments that you've conducted so far and determine which of the following areas each falls into:

- **Work-related experiments:** These include behavioral experiments involving your tasks at work, your interactions with coworkers or your boss, and decisions that involve your job.

- **School-related experiments:** These include experiments involving class assignments, decisions about courses or what topics to write about or study, and interactions with your teachers or classmates.

- **Family- and home-related experiments:** These include experiments involving your home, your family, your health, or the health of loved ones. Examples might be delegating tasks to family members, completing chores without using a pre-planned list, or making decisions about home repairs or renovations.

- **Social experiments:** These include experiments that involve activities with friends, trying out new things (by yourself or with others), making decisions in social situations, or reducing reassurance seeking.

Do most of the behavioral experiments you've done so far fall in only one or two categories? If so, come up with at least three experiments in a category that you haven't worked on or that you've only tried once or twice.

Experiment 1: _____

_____

Experiment 2: _____

_____

Experiment 3: _____

_____

For now, just view this exercise as brainstorming. A bit later in the chapter you'll make lists of new behavioral experiments to try in both the short term and the long term, and you may wish to include some of these experiments there.

Raising the Stakes in Your Behavioral Experiments

Another way to widen the scope of your experiments is to raise the stakes. That is, now that you've completed a number of small experiments, you can start setting up bigger, more challenging experiments. For example, if you tend to worry about travel and one of your previous behavioral experiments was to pack your suitcase on the morning of a short trip instead of packing several days ahead, a new experiment that raises the stakes would be to not make advance plans for one of the days of an upcoming vacation. Or if you have difficulty delegating tasks and your early experiments have involved allowing your children to wash the dishes unsupervised, the next step might be to let them do a larger task, such as preparing a meal for the family (assuming they're old enough).

These types of experiments are considered a step above earlier experiments because the feared outcome seems more severe, making the experiment a bigger risk. For instance, if you pack your suitcase on the same day you take a short trip, your feared outcome is probably that you'd forget something. However, given that it's a short trip, you're likely to view this as less anxiety provoking because you'll be back home soon and can probably manage without a missing item. On the other hand, not planning all of the activities for one day of a vacation may seem more threatening if the feared outcome is that you wouldn't enjoy that day of your vacation and will have wasted your time and money.

EXERCISE 8.2: Developing More Challenging Behavioral Experiments

A good way to come up with more challenging experiments is to review the behavioral experiments you've already conducted. In chapter 7, we encouraged you to start small, with experiments that were moderately anxiety provoking but doable. Now it's time to up the ante. In the space that follows, write down some of the initial experiments you did and, for each one, try to find a similar experiment that's a bit more challenging. (If you'd like to continue using this approach to develop new exercises in the future, you can download copies of this worksheet at http://www.newharbinger.com/31519.) In case it's helpful, we'll begin with a couple of examples.

Initial experiment: *Not reviewing a small assignment that my son completed for his homework.*

Ideas for more challenging experiments: *Not reviewing my son's assignments for a whole week (and then two weeks). Not asking my son what homework he has to do (for a day, a week, and then two weeks).*

Initial experiment: *Turning my phone off for an hour so I can't see whether anyone is calling or texting me.*

Ideas for more challenging experiments: *Leaving my phone at home for several hours while I run errands. Leaving my phone at home for a whole day, or keeping my phone turned off all day.*

Initial experiment: _____

Ideas for more challenging experiments: _____

_____

Initial experiment: _____

Ideas for more challenging experiments: _____

_____

Initial experiment: _____

Ideas for more challenging experiments: _____

_____

Again, just view this exercise as brainstorming. You may want to include these ideas in the lists you'll create shortly of new behavioral experiments to try in both the short term and the long term.

Tailoring Your Experiments to Your Specific Fears

When conducting behavioral experiments, you're testing whether there is, in fact, a negative outcome when you deliberately face the uncertainty in an unpredictable, novel, or ambiguous situation. This targets the underlying theme in GAD: the threat of uncertainty. But even though people with GAD have intolerance of uncertainty in common, your particular fears about uncertainty and negative outcomes are specific to you. What you find most threatening when facing uncertainty might be different from what someone else finds threatening. Therefore, it's a good idea to develop ongoing behavioral experiments that are tailored to your particular fears.

LOSS OF CONTROL

Some people with GAD describe themselves as control freaks and say they feel threatened and anxious whenever they aren't in direct control of a situation. If you have this kind of desire to be in control, examples of situations that might be anxiety provoking include delegating tasks to others, participating in social activities you didn't plan, and allowing other people to make decisions. In all of these cases, you're giving up control of a situation to someone else, so you're much less certain about how or when it will be completed or how it will turn out.

If you find that giving up control is anxiety provoking for you, you might try behavioral experiments that involve deliberately giving up control. For example, you might have a potluck dinner party where you don't know what people will bring, allow someone else to take over one of your usual tasks either at home or at work, or have a loved one make some decisions at home, such as how to reorganize the cupboards or what home renovations to do.

FEAR OF MAKING A MISTAKE

For some people, what's most anxiety provoking about inviting uncertainty into their lives is the possibility that they'll make a mistake. If this is a central fear for you, you probably find it difficult to make decisions of any sort, whether about purchasing items (such as clothes, electronics, or groceries), about the way you complete a task (for example, how to set up your Internet at home), or about social events (such as what to prepare for a dinner party or what movie to see with friends). People who are afraid of making mistakes in unpredictable, novel, or ambiguous situations are often worried that making a wrong choice will waste time, effort, or money (*What if I buy these tulip bulbs for my garden now and find them on sale cheaper later on?*) or that they'll regret their decision afterward and feel terrible.

Common safety behaviors for this fear include reassurance seeking, trying to get as much information as possible before making a decision in order to reduce the chances of making a mistake, procrastinating, and acting impulsively rather than thinking about decisions. Therefore, good behavioral experiments to target this fear include making decisions without seeking reassurance, excessive research, procrastinating, or acting impulsively.

Some people with a fear of making mistakes go back and forth between covering all the bases (seeking reassurance and doing excessive research) and procrastinating or acting impulsively. This makes sense when you consider that there's no right answer for many decisions. For example, if you ask ten people what the best color to paint your walls would be, you might get ten different answers. Sometimes the more information you get about a decision, the more confusing and unclear the right choice for you may become. You might then choose to impulsively make a decision at random, such as buying the first pair of jeans that fit you, so you won't feel responsible for making a poor choice.

If fear of making a choice is a problem for you, a good behavioral experiment is to engage in controlled decision making—getting just a bit of information about a decision before making a deliberate choice. Again, this is a way of finding a middle ground between seeking too much information and making a choice entirely impulsively. For example, if you need to buy a new pair of shoes, your experiment might involve trying on three or four pairs and then purchasing the shoes you like best among those choices.

EXERCISE 8.3: Making Behavioral Experiments an Ongoing Process

Now that you have some ideas about new behavioral experiments you can do—in different areas of life, to increase the challenge level, or to more directly target your fears—you can come up with a list of experiments to try both now and in the future. Because behavioral experiments are designed to investigate the outcome when you face uncertainty as well as your ability to cope with negative outcomes, it's important to continue engaging in them for several weeks. Only through practice can you begin to gather compelling evidence that might change your negative beliefs about uncertainty and its consequences.

In this exercise, you'll compile two lists: new experiments to try in the short term, and other new experiments to try in the long term. For the first, choose experiments that feel more doable. Once you've benefited from your experience with those, you'll be ready to tackle more difficult experiments, from the second list. For both lists, you might use some of the potential new experiments you identified in Exercises 8.1 and 8.2. (To download this worksheet for future use, visit http://www.newharbinger.com/31519.)

New Behavioral Experiments to Conduct Over the Next Few Weeks

Experiment 1: _____

_____

Experiment 2: _____

_____

Experiment 3: _____

_____

Experiment 4: _____

_____

In exercises 8.1 and 8.2, you might have identified some experiments that are a bit too challenging right now. However, remember that where you start is not where you'll end up, so what might seem too challenging now will probably be more feasible in time. With this in mind, use the following space to list some experiments you might like to try in the future, such as taking a trip by yourself or without making any plans, finding a new job, or going back to school.

Experiments to Try Later On

Experiment 1: _____

_____

Experiment 2: _____

_____

Experiment 3: _____

_____

Experiment 4: _____

_____

EXERCISE 8.4: Taking Stock of the Evidence

Once you have several weeks of additional experience in conducting behavioral experiments under your belt, you can begin to really look at the evidence and draw some general conclusions. In exercise 7.2, which you completed after devising and practicing your initial behavioral experiments, you answered some questions about the frequency of positive, negative, and neutral outcomes, the severity of negative outcomes, and your coping ability. Now that you have even more experience to draw on, you can investigate the accuracy of your beliefs more fully, using some similar questions.

Number of experiments conducted: _____

How many outcomes were positive? _____

How many outcomes were neutral? _____

How many outcomes were negative? _____

If some outcomes were negative, how many times were
they as severe or bad as you expected? _____

How many times did you have to cope with a negative outcome? _____

How many times did you find that you coped or dealt with the
situation well? _____

Most of our clients are surprised to find that their negative beliefs about uncertainty are often inaccurate. You might have discovered this yourself. Although negative outcomes do sometimes occur, they aren't nearly as frequent as you may expect. And when there is a negative outcome, it typically isn't that bad. Plus, you might have found that you're quite capable of coping well with most negative outcomes when they arise.

Based on all the work you've done in this chapter and chapter 7, you can also begin to think about your overall impression of the outcome of your behavioral experiments and the impact of these exercises on different aspects of your life. So take some time to think about your experiences over the past several weeks, as you've been doing behavioral experiments to help dispel negative beliefs about uncertainty. Ask yourself the following questions to assist you in taking stock of your experiences:

- Have you noticed any changes in your life since you started doing the experiments?

- Are there some situations that you used to view as threatening that you can now easily enter into?

- If you're engaging in fewer safety behaviors in certain situations, do you notice that you have more free time or that you're able to get things done more quickly?

- Has your opinion of your ability to cope with negative outcomes changed? Do you feel more confident in your ability to navigate unpredictable, novel, and ambiguous situations?

- Do you worry less?

- Have there been any changes or improvements in your physical symptoms of GAD, such as sleep problems, irritability, muscle tension, or feeling restless and keyed up?

- Have others in your life noticed a change in you?

In our experience, although everyone finds behavioral experiments difficult at first, many people report that they quickly become rewarding. You may have a feeling of accomplishment for having tried something new, and you may also have found that the outcomes of certain experiments were surprisingly positive, which suggests that facing uncertainty could have some definite advantages.

Embracing Uncertainty and Seeing Its Benefits

So far you've been working on trying to change your negative beliefs about uncertainty in unpredictable, novel, and ambiguous situations. In essence, your focus has been on tolerating the uncertainties of life. This assumes that feeling uncertain isn't pleasant—that it's just something that, at best, you can learn to live with. But what if being uncertain can be a pleasant state that you might actually learn to embrace in certain situations, rather than merely tolerate?

The fact is, some people thrive amidst the uncertainties of life, enjoying the feeling of flying by the seat of their pants. Why might this be the case? It typically has to do with their relationship to uncertainty or, more specifically, their beliefs about the potential benefits of entering into unpredictable, novel, and ambiguous situations. In the sections that follow, we'll discuss some of the advantages that can arise from embracing uncertainty in certain situations.

Enjoying Spontaneity and New Experiences

Like most people, you've undoubtedly found that you sometimes derive great pleasure from unexpected events in life: finding twenty dollars in an old pair of jeans, unwrapping presents, or meeting someone new and interesting at a social event. These kinds of events are typically unplanned and unexpected, so they arrive as a welcome surprise. In these situations, being spontaneous and not having a plan can give you the opportunity to experience things that you might not normally experience. You might have noticed this in some of your behavioral experiments, particularly if you did something new or unexpected.

This kind of enjoyment shifts unpredictable, novel, and ambiguous situations from purely threatening to potential opportunities. Given that life is inherently uncertain and unexpected situations are inevitable, the ability to spontaneously adapt to these situations can make life much more pleasant in general. A helpful analogy is the idea of swimming in the ocean. It requires a great deal of energy to swim against the waves, and there is always another wave crashing toward you that you have to face. Occasionally allowing yourself to just bob up and down with the waves is much easier, and it also gives you a chance to enjoy the scenery for a bit.

Increased Confidence

As behavioral experiments help you become more accustomed to facing uncertainty, you'll probably notice that you're quite capable of handling problems that arise. For example, if you turned off your phone for a few hours and later found that you'd missed some texts, it's likely that you contacted the people who texted you and handled any situations that arose. Or if you went to the grocery store without a list and forgot to pick up a few items, you probably either went back to the store to pick them up or decided to make do without for the time being.

Most of our clients are surprised at how well they cope with any negative outcomes that arise, and also at how easily or quickly any problems are resolved. This is an important benefit to embracing uncertainty: you get to find out that you're much more capable of facing adversity than you thought you were. Take a moment to consider what you're telling yourself every time you attempt to mentally plan and prepare for any eventuality. You're essentially telling yourself that you're incapable of thinking on your feet and that if you don't have a plan beforehand, you'll be overwhelmed; you're telling yourself that you have no confidence in your ability to cope with negative outcomes. Embracing uncertainty allows you to increase your confidence by observing through direct experience how capable you actually are in difficult situations.

Seeing Through a New Lens

One of the most powerful benefits of embracing uncertainty has to do with changing the lens through which you see the world. If you view the uncertainty of life as something that's negative or, at best, tolerable, you'll have a tendency to see unpredictable, novel, and ambiguous situations through a lens that focuses on all the potential negative outcomes that may occur. As a result, your approach to these situations is one of minimizing harm. For example, if a friend invites you to go somewhere over a long weekend, you're likely to focus on ways to reduce the discomfort of the trip or how to get along with your friend for two or three days straight. In other words, you'll focus on how to reduce the negative aspects of the trip in order to make it as painless as possible.

If, on the other hand, you choose to embrace the uncertainty, your approach will involve maximizing pleasure, with a focus on all the pleasant events that might take place during the trip and how to make it as fun as possible. In this case, you might think about what kind of music you could listen to together, what events or activities the two of you might enjoy, and whether you'll find any interesting souvenirs or gifts to bring back home. When you view the uncertainty in day-to-day situations not as inherently threatening, but as something that could potentially have benefits, your outlook on life changes accordingly.

EXERCISE 8.5: Finding the Positives in Uncertainty

Simply understanding and potentially agreeing with the idea that embracing uncertainty has benefits isn't enough to allow you to adopt this perspective. Only with time and experience—the same principles that underlie behavioral experiments—can you try on this perspective for yourself. As an initial step, it will be helpful to reflect upon the benefits you can envision for yourself if you were to not only tolerate uncertainty but even see it as positive on occasion.

With this in mind, in this exercise we'd like you to give some thought to the advantages of viewing the uncertainties in life as something to embrace. Reflect on the different areas of life listed here and write down any advantages of embracing uncertainty that you've already noticed or that you'd like to experience in the future. We encourage you to do this exercise periodically to revisit the benefits of embracing uncertainty and to identify new ones. (To download a fresh worksheet for that purpose, visit http://www.newharbinger .com/31519.)

Your relationship with friends and loved ones

_____

_____

_____

Your performance and satisfaction at work or school

_____

_____

_____

Your social life

_____

_____

_____

Your health and the health of loved ones

_____

_____

_____

EXERCISE 8.6: Checking In on Your GAD Symptoms

As discussed in the past few chapters, the ultimate goal of challenging your negative beliefs about uncertainty with behavioral experiments is to diminish the sense of threat you feel in unpredictable, novel, and ambiguous situations, and thereby reduce your worry and anxiety. Before you move on to the next chapter, we recommend that you once again fill out the Worry and Anxiety Questionnaire (reprinted with permission from Dugas et al. 2001) to assess your GAD symptoms, this time for a one-month time frame, rather than the six-month time frame in chapter 1. Then you can compare your current responses to those you initially wrote down. Going forward, it would be a good idea to fill out the questionnaire every few months or so in order to see your progress over time. (A downloadable version of the questionnaire can be found at http://www.newharbinger .com/31519.)

WORRY AND ANXIETY QUESTIONNAIRE

1. What subjects do you worry about most often?

   a. _____

   b. _____

   c. _____

   d. _____

   e. _____

   f. _____

   For the following items, please circle the corresponding number (0 to 8).

2. Do your worries seem excessive or exaggerated?

   Not at all   Moderately   Totally
   excessive   excessive   excessive
   0 .... 1 .... 2 .... 3 .... 4 .... 5 .... 6 .... 7 8

3. Over the past month, how many days have you been bothered by excessive worry?

   Never   One day   Every day
                                 out of two
   0 .... 1 .... 2 .... 3 .... 4 .... 5 .... 6 .... 7 8

4. Do you have difficulty controlling your worries? For example, when you start worrying about something, do you have difficulty stopping?

No difficulty   Moderate   Extreme

                                 difficulty   difficulty

0 .... 1 .... 2 .... 3 .... 4 .... 5 .... 6 .... 7 8

5. Over the past month, to what extent have you been disturbed by the following symptoms when you were worried or anxious? Rate each symptom by circling a number (0–8).

a. Restlessness or feeling keyed up or on edge

Not at all   Moderately   Very severely

0 .... 1 .... 2 .... 3 .... 4 .... 5 .... 6 .... 7 8

b. Being easily fatigued

Not at all   Moderately   Very severely

0 .... 1 .... 2 .... 3 .... 4 .... 5 .... 6 .... 7 8

c. Difficulty concentrating or mind going blank

Not at all   Moderately   Very severely

0 .... 1 .... 2 .... 3 .... 4 .... 5 .... 6 .... 7 8

d. Irritability

Not at all   Moderately   Very severely

0 .... 1 .... 2 .... 3 .... 4 .... 5 .... 6 .... 7 8

e. Muscle tension

Not at all   Moderately   Very severely

0 .... 1 .... 2 .... 3 .... 4 .... 5 .... 6 .... 7 8

f. Sleep disturbance (difficulty falling or staying asleep or restless unsatisfying sleep)

Not at all   Moderately   Very severely

0 .... 1 .... 2 .... 3 .... 4 .... 5 .... 6 .... 7 8

6. To what extent does worry or anxiety interfere with your life? For example, your work, social activities, family life, and so on?

Not at all   Moderately   Severe

0 .... 1 .... 2 .... 3 .... 4 .... 5 .... 6 .... 7 8

To meet criteria for GAD, you must endorse the following criteria (check all that apply):

☐   At least two worry topics on item 1

☐   A score of 4 or higher on items 2, 3, 4, and 6

☐   A score of 4 or higher on at least three of the symptoms on item 5

If you checked all three boxes, you meet the criteria required for a diagnosis of GAD.

Taking Stock of Your Progress

At the beginning of this book, you learned that the goal of your work isn't to cure you of GAD, but to reduce your worry and anxiety symptoms so they fall within normal, functional levels. However, do keep in mind that what normal looks like for you might not be the same as what it looks like for someone else. After all, "normal" can cover a very wide range. In addition, because all people with GAD are different, each person's progress is likely to be unique. If you filled out the preceding Worry and Anxiety Questionnaire a second time, hopefully you found that your worries have decreased, that you have fewer anxiety symptoms, and that your GAD symptoms now cause less impairment in your daily life.

Still, some people find that they continue to meet the criteria for a GAD diagnosis at this point, even after engaging in behavioral experiments for several weeks or months. If this is the case for you, don't be discouraged. Since GAD symptoms fall on a continuum of severity, it isn't uncommon for people to discover that although their worries have diminished, they're still significant enough at this point to be above the clinical threshold of an anxiety disorder. And if you were very high on the continuum of severity when you first started working with this book, you may have made significant progress yet still fall within the range of a GAD diagnosis. Remember that the goal is to learn how to manage your worry and anxiety over the long run. Steady progress toward that goal is more important than how long it takes to achieve it.

CHAPTER 9

Coping with Worries About Current Problems

In chapters 5 through 8, we focused on working with the thoughts and actions that lead to worry. Specifically, when you change negative beliefs about uncertainty, you'll be less likely to view unpredictable, novel, and ambiguous situations as threatening, which in turns leads to less worry. Because the content of your worry can change from day to day, working on what sets off your worries (beliefs about uncertainty), rather than the worries themselves, is what will ultimately help you reduce worry over the long run.

Even so, you might find that certain worries keep coming up, despite an overall reduction in your worrying in general. In that case, it can be helpful to have some strategies for dealing with these resistant, "leftover" worries. Therefore, this chapter and the next one will focus on helping you cope with your remaining worries. As you may recall, in chapter 1 we introduced two different types of worry: worries about current problems and worries about hypothetical situations. Not surprisingly, the strategies for coping with each type of worry are different, so we will address them separately. In this chapter, we'll focus on how to manage worries about current problems. In chapter 10, we'll look at how to address worries about hypothetical situations.

Since you probably have lots of experience by now with behavioral experiments designed to test your beliefs about uncertainty, you might find that you worry substantially less than when you first started reading this book. As such, you might not need to work through this chapter or chapter 10. It is therefore a good idea to start by figuring out whether these types of worries are still a problem for you. The next exercise will help you do that.

EXERCISE 9.1: Monitoring Worry Types

To give you a good idea of what specific worries you might still be struggling with, start tracking your worries again, using the Worry Monitoring Log in exercise 1.3 (available for download at http://www.newharbinger.com/31519). After a week or two, look over the worries you've listed and record whether they involve current problems or hypothetical situations.

As a reminder, worries about current problems are concerns about problem situations you're dealing with in the here and now. Examples include worries about finding a job after being laid off, getting appropriate day care for your kids, or difficulty meeting people after moving to a new city. These are situations over which you have some control, so there's something that you can do to deal with the problem. By contrast, worries about hypothetical situations are concerns about situations that might potentially happen in the future. Because they involve worrying about something that hasn't happened yet, you don't really have much control over the situation and therefore can't engage in problem solving. Examples of these situations include developing a disease later in life, coping with the death or serious illness of a loved one in the future, or potentially getting fired from your job.

If your tracking reveals any worries about current problems, list them here. Save any worries that you might have about hypothetical situations for chapter 10.

Worries About Current Problems

1. _____

_____

2. _____

_____

3. _____

_____

4. _____

_____

5. _____

_____

Understanding Problem Solving

As discussed in chapter 3, many people with GAD believe that worry is helpful—that it can provide motivation and be useful in solving problems. However, there's a difference between worrying about problems and actually solving them. Worry is often a passive process that goes on in the mind. You might think about the problem, potential solutions to the problem, and the pros and cons of different courses of action you could take. However, these are just thoughts, not actions to address the problem itself. For example, if you're worried about an exam you failed, you'll probably think about how this will affect your overall grade for the class, and you might mentally review your options: you could talk to the teacher, you could drop the class, or you could plan on studying more for the final in order to boost your average. You might also worry that if you drop the class you'll just have to take it again, or that even with extra study you still won't do well on the final. Thinking about these things might feel productive, but unless you actually address the problem, these worries aren't especially helpful. In fact, you might become so anxious about the situation that you procrastinate or avoid dealing with the problem altogether.

Problem solving is a practical alternative to worrying about problems. It's an active strategy that allows you to deal with a problem situation and achieve a resolution. It's comprised of two distinct yet related components: your orientation to or attitudes about problems and problem solving, and your actual problem-solving skills. Regarding problem orientation—the set of attitudes you have about problems and problem solving—research has shown that although people with GAD have the same knowledge of problem-solving skills as others, they're more likely to have a *negative problem orientation*, or negative beliefs about problems and their problem-solving ability (Dugas et al. 1998). This negative attitude can in turn interfere with a person's use of problem-solving skills (D'Zurilla and Nezu 2007). So even though you're probably just as good at solving problems as anyone else, you probably have a negative view of your problems and of yourself as a problem solver, which is likely to lead you to avoid your problems rather than dealing with them. Learning how to effectively solve problems in daily life instead of worrying about them therefore involves addressing both parts of problem solving: problem orientation and the practical application of problem-solving skills.

Understanding Negative Problem Orientation

A negative problem orientation includes three primary attitudes: the tendency to view problems as threatening; doubts about your ability to solve problems; and pessimism about the outcome of potential solutions (D'Zurilla and Nezu 2007; Robichaud and Dugas 2005). In other words, if you have a negative problem orientation, you might say to yourself, *I don't like problems, I'm not good at solving them, and even when I do, things don't turn out well.* Let's look at how this can affect your ability to solve problems.

Consequences of a Negative Problem Orientation

Similar to what happens when you have negative beliefs about uncertainty, holding negative attitudes about problems and problem solving has a significant impact on your thoughts, feelings, and behaviors. As an example, let's say you worry about where to take your family on an upcoming vacation, and that your budget is tight. You want everyone to have a good time, but your family members have very different interests. If you have a negative problem orientation, you may feel threatened by trying to figure out this problem, think you won't be able to come up with any good ideas, and think anything you come up with won't work out (perhaps the vacation will be too expensive or not everyone in your family will have a good time). How will these thoughts about your problem impact you?

Effects on feelings. Whenever you start to think about this problem, you'll probably feel anxious, frustrated, and irritated because the situation seems overwhelming and potentially unsolvable.

Effects on behaviors. Because you see problems as very threatening, you might avoid the problem or procrastinate about solving it. If so, you may end up spending more energy on trying not to deal with the problem than on actually solving it, especially if you're feeling anxious or frustrated by the situation.

Effects on thoughts. An obvious effect on your thoughts is that you keep worrying about the problem. In addition, as time passes small problems can become larger ones and can even create new problems, which then lead to new worries and thoughts about how to solve them. If you avoid the problem of picking a vacation spot, it might become a bigger issue, and more expensive, as time goes on. In this example, the cost of flights might increase, and there could be limited space in local hotels. You might start to have problems figuring out how to pay for the trip, in which case your finances would become an additional worry on top of your worries about the vacation.

In essence, having a negative problem orientation leads to more negative emotions, more worries, and greater avoidance of problems. But remember, research shows that people with GAD have the same knowledge of problem-solving skills as anyone else. So although a negative problem orientation makes you less likely to actually solve your problems, this isn't because you don't have the ability to solve them; it's because you don't think you can.

Negative Problem Orientation and Intolerance of Uncertainty

Why is it that people with GAD are more likely to have a negative problem orientation? The answer lies in the nature of problems themselves. Problems in daily life involve situations with a potential negative outcome for which there isn't a clear or obvious solution. In other words, these problems lead to a state of uncertainty because the outcome is unpredictable, as is the effectiveness of a particular solution, which triggers worry and feelings of threat.

The impact that intolerance of uncertainty has on problem solving shows how negative beliefs about uncertainty can have pervasive effects across multiple aspects of your life. It also illustrates the importance of ongoing behavioral experiments to challenge those beliefs. In fact, because of the uncertainty inherent in problems, you can view problem solving as a type of behavioral experiment in which you get to find out how you really handle problems when they arise.

Challenging Negative Problem Orientation

Since negative problem orientation can have a strong impact on whether and how you use your problem-solving skills, it's important to challenge these attitudes before moving forward with problem solving. However, as with beliefs about uncertainty and beliefs about the usefulness of worry, changing your ideas about problems and problem solving can't be accomplished by simply thinking positively or trying to tell yourself that your problems aren't threatening and that you're a good problem-solver. Rather, the goal is to develop strategies for recognizing problems as soon as they come up, to look at problems in a more balanced way, and ultimately to use your direct experience to obtain evidence about your ability to solve problems.

Recognizing Problems Early

Because people with GAD often procrastinate or avoid dealing with their problems, they're less likely to recognize them when they first arise. But as mentioned, when small problems aren't dealt with, they can become big problems over time, making it more challenging to deal with them. There are two strategies that can improve your ability to recognize problems earlier and deal with them as soon as possible: using your emotions as a cue, and developing a list of recurrent problems.

USING YOUR EMOTIONS AS A CUE

A common mistake many people make is misinterpreting their negative emotions as the problem in difficult situations. However, negative emotions are usually the consequence of a problem, not the problem itself. For example, if you're consistently stressed and anxious at the end of your workday, the problem might not be the fact that you're stressed and anxious. Instead, the problem might be something at work, such as not completing tasks on time or having difficulties with coworkers, that's making you feel stressed. If you keep this in mind, you can use negative emotions as a cue, alerting you to observe your environment and determine whether there's a problem. In addition to helping you catch problems earlier, before they become more serious, it will also allow you to view your emotions in a less negative way and actually see them as helpful for identifying problems in your life.

EXERCISE 9.2: Emotion Monitoring for Problem Detection

Learning to use your emotions as a cue is a skill that requires some practice. We recommend taking a few days to monitor your emotions and be an observer of your own experience. The following worksheet will help you track your negative emotions, the situations in which they occur, and whether or not you can identify a particular problem within the situation. Over the next few days, fill it out anytime you detect negative emotions, particularly those that have a bearing on your worry and anxiety. As with some of the other monitoring forms in this book, the information you gather will be most useful if you fill out the form as soon as possible after you detect a negative emotion. When describing the situation, asking yourself a few key questions can be helpful: Who was with you? Where were you? What was happening? To fill in the "Problem" column, consider whether there was a trigger for your negative feelings. Can you identify a particular problem within the situation?

Here's an example to show you how it works, followed by a blank form for your use. (A downloadable version of the blank form is available at http://www.newharbinger.com/31519.)

SAMPLE PROBLEM TRACKING LOG

Negative emotion	Situation	Problem?
Nervous and irritated	*Getting ready in the morning while also getting the kids ready for school. I left late for work, and I snapped at the kids when they were slow in eating their breakfast.*	*Yes. There doesn't seem to be enough time in the morning to get myself and the kids ready to leave the house on time.*
Frustrated	*Trying to complete some overdue reports at work. I'm having a hard time understanding all of the requirements for completing them.*	*Yes. My boss has changed the requirements for completing reports, and I don't feel the changes were properly explained to me.*
Sad and lonely	*I'm at home alone on the weekend and I don't have any plans. My friends are all busy with their own plans.*	*Yes. My social life is very limited. I'd like to be more socially active, but I don't know how.*

Problem Tracking Log

Negative emotion	Situation	Problem?

DEVELOPING A LIST OF RECURRING PROBLEMS

In addition to tracking your emotions in order to identify problems early, you can also keep a list of problems as they come up, with a focus on those that come up repeatedly. The problems that cause people the most distress are often the ones that keep coming up again and again. This usually happens either because they didn't solve the problem previously, or because the solution they came up with wasn't effective in the long term. For example, you might find that at the end of each month you have problems paying all of your bills, which suggests that managing your finances is a recurrent problem. By keeping a list of recurrent problems, you can see whether certain issues seem to arise repeatedly. If so, this lets you know that your solutions to certain problems aren't working well, and also allows you to prepare for the situation more effectively the next time, rather than being surprised.

EXERCISE 9.3: Recurring Problems List

Take some time now to think about whether certain problems tend to come up repeatedly. If so, list those problems here. You may find it helpful to keep an ongoing list of recurring problems, perhaps in a journal or electronic device.

1. _____

2. _____

3. _____

4. _____

5. _____

6. _____

Seeing the Opportunity in Problems

It's human nature to try to avoid situations that we see as threatening and to approach those that seem like opportunities. Of course, one result of this dynamic is that when you view problems as threatening, it decreases the chances that you'll try to work on solving them. Plus, if you're going to work at anything, you're more likely to persevere if you see some type of opportunity or reward that would justify putting forth the effort. This is why it's important to try to find the opportunities in problem situations.

A good first step is to realize that threats and opportunities can be seen as two extremes on a single continuum. Problem situations are rarely 100 percent threatening or 100 percent an opportunity. Rather, most problems in daily life lie somewhere between those two extremes. You'll probably always see problems as somewhat threatening, which makes sense given that dealing with problems isn't fun. However, there are often opportunities that can make approaching a problem situation beneficial. For example, let's say you had a big argument with a friend, and she's still very angry with you. Attempting to deal with this situation would probably feel threatening; you may worry that she'll yell at you or be unwilling to work things out. However, there are also opportunities in this problem. For example, if you address the issues with your friend, you might be able to make your friendship stronger in the long run. You could also improve your own communication skills, which might help you better deal with disagreements with others later on. Neither of these opportunities eliminates the threats from this problem, but they do allow you to have a balanced view of the situation, which can help you feel less overwhelmed and anxious when starting to think about the problem-solving process.

EXERCISE 9.4: Finding Opportunities in Problems

To help you practice finding the opportunities within problems, use the problems you identified in the Problem Tracking Log in exercise 9.2, as well as your list of recurring problems. For this exercise, choose a problem that's particularly troublesome for you and describe it briefly. Rate how threatening the situation seems to you using a scale from 0 to 100 percent threatening. You can then try to come up with realistic opportunities that the situation might hold for you. One key guideline: Only list opportunities that make sense to you. If you don't believe what you're writing, it won't be helpful.

After you've written down a few opportunities, rerate how threatening the situation now seems to you, again from 0 to 100 percent. You won't always find opportunities that make the situation feel less threatening, but by looking at the complete picture you can usually develop a more fair and balanced view of the situation, as shown in the example. (If you find this approach helpful, you can download additional forms for this exercise at http://www.newharbinger.com/31519.)

Sample problem: *My son's school is unexpectedly closed for the day, and I don't have anyone to babysit him while I'm at work.*

Threat rating: *100 percent threatening*

Opportunities: *I might be able to find child care options in my area other than a babysitter so I'll be prepared if this happens again. I could also improve my communication with my boss and clarify how to handle unexpected situations that might keep me from coming in to work at the last minute.*

New threat rating: *70 percent threatening*

Problem: _____

Threat rating (0 to 100%): _____

Opportunities: _____

_____

_____

New threat rating (0 to 100%): _____

Problem: _____

Threat rating (0 to 100%): _____

Opportunities: _____

_____

_____

New threat rating (0 to 100%): _____

Moving Toward Problem Solving

The negative problem orientation strategies presented in the preceding sections aren't designed to radically change your attitudes about problems and problem solving. Rather, the purpose is to make the transition into actual problem solving a little less anxiety provoking or overwhelming. When you actually start solving problems, you can begin to directly test some of your negative beliefs: Are all of your problems as threatening as you thought? Is it actually true that you do a poor job of solving problems? Do all of your solutions really turn out negatively? You can discover the answers to these questions by actively engaging in problem solving.

We all deal with problems on a daily basis, most of which are easily and quickly solved. For example, if you oversleep and are late for work, you might decide to skip breakfast and call your boss to let her know you'll be a few minutes late. The majority of minor problems are resolved by doing what first comes to mind or whatever you've typically done in the past. However, problems that lead to significant worry and distress aren't so easy to address. Often there's no obvious solution, and whatever you've already done in an attempt to deal with the problem either didn't work or only worked in the short term. These types of problems require a more deliberate problem-solving approach. To that end, the rest of this chapter focuses on how to resolve more challenging problems by using effective problem-solving skills.

Applying Problem-Solving Skills

You probably already know the steps required to solve a problem: you define your problem, set goals, think about potential solutions, decide which solution is best for your problem, and then carry it out. However, having knowledge about the skills needed to solve a problem is different from actually applying those skills in your daily life. In fact, most people with GAD are excellent problem solvers...for other people's problems! Where they struggle is in applying those skills to their own problems.

One reason people have difficulty applying problem-solving skills to their own problems is loss of perspective. You're more likely to feel distressed and anxious when you think about your problems, which can make you less objective. Although you might empathize with other people's problems, you don't feel the same sense of personal distress, which allows you to maintain greater objectivity. It's a bit like the difference between being in a maze as opposed to seeing it from above: you can see the whole picture when you look down on a maze.

As noted, there are several steps in effective problem solving (see Nezu, Nezu, and D'Zurilla 2007 for a detailed and user-friendly description of problem solving):

1. Defining the problem

2. Formulating a goal

3. Generating solutions

4. Making a decision

5. Implementing a solution and assessing its effectiveness

In the sections that follow, we'll go through each step in detail, using this sample problem throughout:

You've been unemployed for several months now. You've applied for a number of jobs in your field, but you either don't have the right qualifications and training, or you don't get a job offer after the interview. You're living on your savings now, but they'll run out in the next month or two.

Step 1: Defining the Problem

One of the most important steps of problem solving is defining the problem, as it will influence all of the subsequent steps. Here are some guidelines for defining the problem in a helpful way.

FOCUS ON THE FACTS

Make sure that your definition is based on observable facts (who, what, where, and when), and that it's specific and concrete. It's common for people to make assumptions, which may be untrue, and which can also make the definition of the problem confusing. For example, if you define the problem as "People don't like me in job interviews," it would be difficult to know whether this is true (how do you know people don't like you?) and it would also be difficult to set goals (how much do people need to like you?).

FIND THE PRIMARY OBSTACLE

Challenging problems typically involve the presence of an obstacle between what the situation currently is and how you'd like it to be. Identifying the primary obstacle is one of the main challenges of defining the problem. It can be helpful to initially write out your definition by describing the current situation, your desired situation, and the obstacle between the two—in other words, what's preventing you from attaining the desired situation:

- What is the current situation? *I'm unemployed.*

- What would you like the situation to be? *I'd like to have a job in my field.*

- What is the obstacle? *There currently are no jobs in my field that I'm qualified for.*

From there, you can write out the problem in one sentence: *The problem is that I'd like a job in my field, but there are currently no jobs in my field that I'm qualified for.*

The problem can be quite different depending on how you describe your current and ideal situations. For example, consider the difference if you had answered the questions in the following way:

- What is the current situation? *I'm running out of money from my savings.*

- What would you like the situation to be? *I'd like to pay my bills and start saving money.*

- What is the obstacle? *I currently don't have a job.*

In this case, your definition of the problem situation would be distinctly different: *The problem is that I want to have money to pay my bills and start saving, but I don't have a job.*

In the first example, the primary obstacle is difficulty finding work in your field, while in the second example, the primary obstacle is financial. Neither one of these definitions of the problem is incorrect, but as you can see, each will have a major impact on your goals and potential solutions, so it's important to identify what the primary issue is for you.

DON'T BE TOO NARROW IN SCOPE

One of the difficulties many people face when trying to define the problem is that they have a very specific outcome in mind that becomes woven into the definition. For example, you might describe the problem in the following way: "I want to have a job that pays at least forty dollars per hour, is in my field, and is close to my home." This definition is so specific and narrow that your options will be very limited. If instead you said, "I want to find a job in my field" or "I want a job that pays enough to cover my bills," you would widen the scope of the problem, making it more likely that you can come up with lots of different potential solutions.

Step 2: Formulating a Goal

Once you've properly defined your problem, it's important to have a clear idea of what a positive outcome would look like for you. Therefore, the second step of problem solving is identifying clear goals that flow naturally from your definition of the problem. For example, if you defined the problem as a lack of jobs in your field that you're qualified for, one of your goals might be to obtain more experience or education. However, if you defined the problem as a lack of money to pay bills, your goals might be to get any type of job that would give you enough money to cover all your bills. Here are some guidelines for effectively setting goals.

SET CONCRETE AND SPECIFIC GOALS

A common mistake is not setting clearly observable goals, which can make it a challenge to know when you've achieved them. For example, if one of your goals is "feeling confident in interviews," how will you know when you've achieved this goal? Because the goal involves a feeling, it's difficult to measure. Similarly, a goal of "having more money" also isn't very specific: How much is "more money"? Effective goals allow you to see your progress and know when you've achieved them. For example, "having enough money to cover my rent and my utilities each month" and "being offered a job of any kind in the next two months" are specific and concrete goals that have observable outcomes.

SET REALISTIC GOALS

Because problem solving can be a challenging process, you want to maximize your chances of success. If you set goals that you're unlikely to reach, you might end up feeling demoralized. So choose goals that are reasonably achievable. For example, you might like to be offered a very high-paying job at the top company in your field, but if you don't have much experience, this goal probably isn't realistic.

DIFFERENTIATE BETWEEN SHORT-TERM AND LONG-TERM GOALS

For some problems, you might decide to set multiple goals. This is a particularly good course of action when you probably can't achieve your main goal in the short term. For example, if one of your goals is "having five thousand dollars in savings," this probably isn't a goal you can achieve right away, especially if you aren't currently employed. However, you might set several short-term goals, such as "getting a full-time job" and "setting aside at least one hundred dollars a month," that can help you achieve your long-term goal.

Step 3: Generating Solutions

One of the main reasons why it can be so difficult to deal with challenging problems is that there's a tendency to come up with the same solutions you've used in the past. However, those old familiar solutions probably didn't work in the first place, so it's important to come up with new ideas. A good way to do this is to use the three principles of brainstorming: deferring judgment, generating many potential solutions, and generating a variety of ideas.

PRINCIPLE 1: DEFER JUDGMENT

The best way to come up with new and creative solutions is to write down any ideas that cross your mind without judging them. It's common for people to censor themselves when thinking about solutions, ruling out alternatives right away because they don't seem like good ideas. Therefore, the first principle of brainstorming is to allow yourself to write down any and all solutions that come to mind, including those that seem silly or unrealistic. Using the sample problem, this might include solutions like playing the lottery, opening your own company, or moving out of your apartment to live in the woods so as to save money on rent and other bills. These solutions might sound off-the-wall, but they can help you come up with new ideas, and they can sometimes be modified to produce more realistic solutions. For example, instead of living in the woods to reduce expenses, you might get a smaller apartment or get a roommate.

PRINCIPLE 2: GENERATE QUANTITY

The second principle of brainstorming is to come up with as many solutions as possible. The more potential solutions you have, the more likely you are to find at least one good solution among them. Try to come up with at least ten different solutions. If you're having a hard time thinking up new ideas, ask others for suggestions.

PRINCIPLE 3: GENERATE VARIETY

When brainstorming, it's also important to come up with lots of different types of ideas. The principle of variety means your solutions shouldn't all be variations on the same idea. For example, solutions such as applying for jobs at fast-food restaurants, applying at coffee shops, and applying at convenience stores are all within the same category: looking for jobs in the service industry.

FOCUS ON SOLUTIONS THAT ARE BEHAVIORS

Here's a final guideline on generating solutions: the best potential solutions are those that can be clearly carried out. So try to formulate solutions that reflect a specific course of action, rather than general strategies. For example, let's say one of your solutions is to improve your interview skills. Although this isn't a bad idea, it's unclear how you'll actually carry it out because it's expressed as a strategy. Restating it as a behavior could include having a friend ask you practice interview questions, or contacting people who interviewed you in the past to get specific feedback from them. Therefore, after you've generated a list of potential solutions, read through all of your alternatives and revise as needed so they're expressed as concrete behaviors.

Step 4: Making a Decision

Making a decision can be the trickiest step for people with GAD, since they have a tendency to want to make sure they choose the "right" or "perfect" solution. This leads to getting stuck at this stage, reviewing each option again and again without picking one. So consider this step to be a two-part process: first you evaluate your solutions to determine which ones seem most appropriate for your problem, and then you need to go ahead and make a decision and move on to the next step of problem solving.

It's a good idea to have some criteria you can use to judge which of your solutions are more appropriate. The following four questions will help.

WILL THIS SOLUTION SOLVE MY PROBLEM?

This seems obvious, but because one principle of brainstorming when generating solutions is to defer judgment, you may have come up with solutions that won't directly address the problem or help you reach your goals. For example, one of your solutions might be to go back to school to get more training. If your goal is to get a job in your field, this solution might increase your chances of reaching that goal in the long term, once you're out of school. But if your goal is to start earning money to pay your bills, this solution probably won't solve your problem.

HOW MUCH TIME AND EFFORT IS INVOLVED?

Some solutions will require a great deal more time and effort than others. For example, alternatives like going back to school or moving to a new city where there are more jobs in your field both require a significant amount of time, effort, and expense. This doesn't rule out these ideas. However, you should weigh the time, effort, and expense along with other criteria when choosing the best solution.

HOW WILL I FEEL IF I CHOOSE THIS SOLUTION?

Some solutions may have emotional consequences that make them better or worse choices for you. For example, if one alternative is to borrow money from family and friends, you might decide that this would make you feel guilty, whereas going back to school might make you feel happy and nervous at the same time. Again, negative emotional consequences don't necessarily rule out a solution, but they should be a factor in your decision-making process.

WHAT ARE THE IMPACTS OF THIS SOLUTION IN THE SHORT TERM AND THE LONG TERM?

Finally, it's important to weigh the pros and cons of a solution both for you and for your friends and family in both the short term and the long term. For example, moving to a new city might have a number of advantages for you in both the short term and the long term: it could help you get a job in your field, advance in your career, allow you to pay your bills, and potentially build your savings over time. However, it might also have a number of disadvantages for you and your loved ones: you'd have to leave your home and move somewhere unfamiliar, there's no guarantee that you'll find a job, you'll miss your friends and family, they'll miss you, and you'll have to make new friends.

WEIGHING THE CHOICES

Once you've answered the preceding questions, you're ready to make a choice. As you do so, remember that the primary objective of this step is to pick the best choice you can identify for your problem, not the perfect one. In reality, any solution you choose will probably have some disadvantages. Therefore, don't rule out potential solutions that have some negative aspects. Instead, weigh your answers to each of the four preceding questions and then decide which solution is most promising. Here are a couple of examples:

Potential solution 1: *Move to a new city to find a job in my field.*

Will this solution solve my problem? *Provided that I get offered a job in another city before moving there, this solution could definitely solve my problem.*

How much time and effort is involved? *This solution involves a huge amount of time and effort, since I'd have to find a city where there are jobs in my field, move there, and find a new place to live.*

How will I feel if I choose this solution? *I think I'd feel very nervous and anxious if I move somewhere new since I'm not sure what to expect, but I'm also excited at the possibility of living somewhere new.*

What are the impacts of this solution in the short term and long term? *This solution could be great for my career in the long term. However, I'd miss my family and friends, and it might be difficult to make new friends.*

Potential solution 2: *Borrow money from friends and family.*

Will this solution solve my problem? *This could solve my immediate problem of paying my bills, but it doesn't help me get a job or take care of future expenses.*

How much time and effort is involved? *This solution involves minimal time and effort. The only thing I would have to do is set aside time to speak with people about borrowing money.*

How will I feel if I choose this solution? *I think I would feel pretty bad about asking other people for money.*

What are the impacts of this solution in the short term and long term? *This solution could potentially have a negative personal and social impact on me. My friends and family might not like being asked to give me money, and if I need to ask them to borrow more money in the future, I could jeopardize my relationships. On the plus side, having money right away to take care of my bills would definitely help reduce my stress about finances.*

PICKING A SOLUTION AND MOVING FORWARD

After weighing out your potential solutions, choose the one that seems to be most appropriate for your problem. Remember, you probably won't find a perfect solution. If there were a perfect choice without any negative consequences, it's likely that you would have already found it. Then, once you've chosen a solution, it's extremely important to keep moving forward in the problem-solving process by beginning the next step:

implementing your solution. This will probably be anxiety provoking, given that you have no guarantees about the outcome of your solution. However, as with conducting behavioral experiments, the only way you can find out if your solution will be successful is to follow through on your decision.

Step 5: Implementing a Solution and Assessing Its Effectiveness

This final step in problem solving—implementing a solution—involves two components: planning and carrying out your chosen solution, and then verifying whether your solution is actually working. To implement your solution, write out the exact steps you'll need to carry out. For example, if your choice is to go back to school to get more training, the steps for this choice might include the following:

1. Look up which schools offer the training you need.

2. Inquire about fees, start dates, and prerequisites.

3. Apply to your chosen program.

4. Apply for a student loan (if needed).

5. Register for classes.

Because many people tend to procrastinate when it comes to actually carrying out their chosen solution, writing out clear, concrete steps is a good idea. This will increase the likelihood that you'll follow through.

The final component of implementing a solution is to assess the effectiveness of your solution to see whether it's working as planned. Even the best solutions sometimes don't work out as expected, so it's important to have a way of verifying whether you're moving toward your goals. To do so, you need to have clear and concrete markers for tracking your progress. In this example, if your chosen solution is to go back to school, a marker might be your grades when you go back to school or the amount of hands-on training you receive. If, on the other hand, you decided to get a roommate to share costs, a clear marker would be a decrease in your monthly debt.

The markers you set to track your progress provide helpful information no matter what the outcome and also dictate your final steps. If your markers show that your solution is working as planned, we strongly recommend that you reward yourself in some way, such as taking some time to engage in a pleasant activity. Because problem solving can be challenging, it's helpful and motivating to take the time to praise yourself for a job well done.

If, however, your markers show that your solution isn't working out as planned, you might need to work through the earlier steps again. Did you define the problem well? Were your goals realistic and achievable? Did you come up with lots of different solutions for your problem? Was there an alternative solution that might be more effective for your problem? Did you carry out all of the steps of your solution? It's common to have to review earlier steps and make adjustments. If this is the case for you, be sure to reward yourself for your efforts after working through the problem-solving process once again.

EXERCISE 9.5: Solving One of Your Own Problems

Now that you have guidelines for effective problem solving, you can begin to go through the preceding steps for one of your own problems. The following questions will guide you through each step. In general, challenging problems are best dealt with using pen and paper or typing, since the act of writing gets you out of your head, where worries reside, and engaged in a concrete action. (If you'd like to use this approach for additional problems, you can download the following worksheet at http://www.newharbinger .com/31519.)

Start by writing out one of your worries about a current problem. You can use one of the worries that you identified in exercise 9.1.

Worry about a current problem: _____

_____

Step 1: Defining the Problem

For this step, remember the three key guidelines: 1. Focus on the facts and don't make assumptions. 2. Identify the primary obstacle. 3. Don't be too narrow when defining the scope of the problem.

What is the current situation? _____

_____

What would you like the situation to be? _____

_____

What is the obstacle? _____

_____

Define the problem in one sentence: _____

_____

Step 2: Formulating a Goal

Your goals should be concrete, specific, realistic, and achievable. You can have just one goal or multiple goals, and both short-term and long-term goals. If one goal is long-term, at least one should be short-term, as a stepping-stone along the way.

Goal 1: _____

_____

Goal 2: _____

_____

Goal 3: _____

_____

Goal 4: _____

_____

Step 3: Generating Solutions

Write out as many potential solutions as you can come up with. Follow the three principles of brainstorming: 1. Defer judgment (silly solutions are good!). 2. Generate quantity, coming up with at least ten solutions. 3. Generate variety, coming up with as many different types of solutions as you can. After you've listed your solutions, review them and make sure they involve concrete behaviors, rather than general strategies.

1. _____

2. _____

3. _____

4. _____

5. _____

6. _____

7. _____

8. _____

9. _____

10. _____

Step 4: Making a Decision

Now it's time to choose a solution. For each potential solution, ask yourself the following questions.

1. Will this solve my problem?

2. How much time and effort is involved?

3. How will I feel if I choose this solution?

4. What are the personal and social impacts of this solution in the short term and the long term?

After weighing the solutions based on your responses to those questions, pick the solution that seems best for your problem. Remember, there may not be a perfect solution.

Chosen solution: _____

_____

Step 5: Implementing a Solution and Assessing Its Effectiveness

Now it's time to implement your solution. Begin by listing all of the steps you need to take to carry out your chosen solution. Remember, these steps should be clear and concrete.

Step 1: _____

Step 2: _____

Step 3: _____

Step 4: _____

Step 5: _____

Identify at least one marker that will let you know whether your solution is working or not:

_____

Once you've gone through the steps, assess whether your solution is working. If it is, reward yourself! If it isn't, go through the steps again, then reward yourself for doing that.

Benefits of Problem Solving

As suggested at the beginning of this chapter, engaging in problem solving can help you directly evaluate any beliefs you have about the usefulness of worry as an aid in problem solving. Once you've worked through all of the steps of problem solving, take a moment to reflect on and compare the difference between worrying about problems and actually trying to solve them. Of course, things often don't turn out as planned, but most of our clients report a sense of achievement and pride in taking action to deal with the problems in their lives, no matter how things turned out.

As you worked through this chapter, you might have found that you didn't even need to complete all of the steps in the problem-solving process. Many of our clients report that once they write down their problem and really think about what they hope to achieve, they realize that the problem can be resolved relatively quickly. Others report that they decided to do a behavioral experiment to address their problem instead. Whatever the case may be for you, we hope that you were able to see the difference between directly tackling your problems and being caught in a spin cycle in your mind.

CHAPTER 10

Coping with Worries About Hypothetical Situations

In the previous chapter, you learned how to manage any remaining worries that involve current problems. Now we'll provide a strategy for worries about hypothetical situations—potential problems that haven't happened and may never happen. This can include worries about a loved one getting sick or being in an accident, potentially losing your job, finding yourself alone and isolated later in life, or not having enough money when you eventually retire. Unlike current problems, where there's usually something you can do to resolve the situation, you typically have little or no control over potential problems. Therefore, using problem solving with these types of worries isn't very helpful. It's a bit like pressing the gas pedal on a car that's up on a hydraulic lift: all you're doing is spinning your wheels and getting nowhere.

That said, everyone worries about bad things happening in the future from time to time. The idea of getting fired, experiencing an earthquake, or getting into a serious accident is scary for everyone, and these thoughts cross everyone's mind on occasion. Such worries aren't considered excessive if they remain at the back of your mind when there's no particular reason to worry about them. As discussed in earlier chapters, the problem isn't the presence of worries about future negative events; the problem is your reactions to those thoughts. Specifically, if you're using various mental strategies to try to control your worries, these strategies may be paradoxically increasing the frequency and severity of your worries and keeping them front and center in your thoughts.

Of course, as mentioned at the beginning of chapter 9, your work with this book may have alleviated a great deal of your worry. Therefore, you may no longer have significant or excessive worries about hypothetical situations. Before getting started with this chapter, you might need to verify whether these types of worries are still a problem for you. The next exercise will help you do that.

EXERCISE 10.1: Do You Worry About Hypothetical Situations?

To give you a good idea of whether you're still be struggling with worries about hypothetical situations, you can review the Worry Monitoring Log you filled out for exercise 9.1. Alternatively, you can track your worries again using a blank Worry Monitoring Log (available for download at http://www.newharbinger.com/31519); then after a week or two, look over the worries you've listed and identify any that involve hypothetical situations.

As a reminder, everyone has worries about hypothetical situations at times. So before listing your worries, consider whether they're excessive, meaning you dwell on them frequently or without good reason, and whether they're at the forefront of your thoughts. For example, if you worry about earthquakes on a daily basis without any earthquake warnings being issued for your area, this worry would be excessive. With this in mind, consider whether any of your remaining worries about hypothetical situations are excessive. If so, list them here.

Worries About Hypothetical Situations

1. _____

_____

2. _____

_____

3. _____

_____

4. _____

_____

5. _____

_____

Understanding Fear

Before we discuss how reactions to worries about hypothetical situations can unintentionally increase the frequency of worry, it's important to understand how fear works. To make the principles of fear easy to understand, we'll use a specific and concrete fear: the fear of elevators. There are three main ways to cope with this fear: avoidance, neutralizing the fear, or facing the fear.

Avoidance of Fear

One way to cope with a fear of elevators is to simply avoid them and take the stairs instead. This coping mechanism allows you to avoid both the "dangers" of being in an elevator (for example, it could get stuck, malfunction, or crash with you inside) and the uncomfortable feelings of anxiety you experience when riding an elevator. The problem with this approach is that although it immediately reduces catastrophic thoughts about riding in elevators and the associated anxiety, it doesn't reduce your fear of being in an elevator. In fact, it increases your fear because it allows you to believe something bad would have happened if you had taken the elevator. Therefore, the next time you're confronted with taking an elevator, your catastrophic thoughts (*Elevators are so dangerous*) and your anxiety will return. As discussed in earlier chapters, avoidance maintains fears in the long term, so strategies involving avoidance are ultimately ineffective, yet they compel you to use them every time you face a feared situation.

Neutralizing Fear

Let's say that instead of avoiding elevators, you decide to face your fear and ride in one. Once you're in the elevator, you'll probably begin to have thoughts about it getting stuck or crashing, and your anxiety will start to rise. You might then decide to close your eyes or imagine you're somewhere else. Or perhaps you've asked a friend to accompany you. All of these strategies are safety behaviors, and they would probably help reduce your catastrophic thoughts and uncomfortable feelings of anxiety somewhat, but not entirely. In other words, they help neutralize, or diminish, your worry and anxiety in the situation.

As we discussed earlier in chapter 6, the problem with these types of safety behaviors is that you never get to see how you'd cope with being in an elevator without using them. You're unable to learn anything new about how dangerous it actually is to ride in an elevator. You also don't get to find out what would happen to your anxiety if you didn't use a safety behavior. Many people fear that if they don't do something to neutralize or dampen their anxiety, it will keep rising until they lose control or become overwhelmed. These safety behaviors are therefore a subtle form of avoidance because you aren't directly facing your fears but instead are trying to neutralize the situation.

Put simply, using safety behaviors interferes with new learning about feared situations. Because of this, you'll continue to be afraid of elevators. As such, although using safety behaviors to reduce your catastrophic thoughts and anxiety can make the feared situation seem more manageable, you haven't reduced your fear; you've simply come up with ways to reduce your menacing thoughts and dampen your anxiety in the moment.

Facing Fears

Another way to cope with your fear of elevators is to face the fear directly, taking the elevator without using any safety behaviors. If you were to do this, you'd probably experience many different thoughts about the dangers of riding an elevator, and your anxiety would be quite high. However, facing your fears, rather than avoiding them or attempting to neutralize them, will give you the opportunity to learn new things about the feared situation and the anxiety that goes along with it.

Let's start with the situation itself: Unless you have extraordinarily bad luck, the chances are high that your elevator ride will be smooth and uneventful, which will allow you to start thinking differently about the probability of getting stuck in an elevator or the elevator crashing to the ground. On the other hand, if you did have some bad luck, you might get stuck in the elevator for a while. (We'll use that example here, given how extremely unlikely it is that the elevator will crash to the ground.) In this case, you might begin to think differently about the dangerousness of being stuck. It would probably be quite upsetting at first; after a while, it might become boring. But it probably wouldn't be as horrible as you originally thought. In addition, you might begin to rethink your ability to cope with the situation without using safety behaviors. You'd probably try calling for help on your cell phone, press the emergency button in the elevator, and then simply wait for help to come, all of which would suggest that you're coping quite well, given the situation. Thus, by confronting your fear without using safety behaviors, you could begin to reevaluate the probability and dangerousness of a negative outcome, as well as your ability to cope with the negative outcome should it occur.

Now let's look at what you might learn about your anxiety if you were to confront your fear without using safety behaviors. First, you'd learn that anxiety has a ceiling. Although it can get quite high, it won't keep rising; rather, it will reach a peak and level off. You'd also learn that anxiety eventually runs out of gas. If you allow yourself to sit with anxiety, it will eventually start to gradually decrease. Both of these properties of anxiety are biological facts; this is simply how anxiety works in the body. And given that anxiety is part of the fight-or-flight system, it isn't surprising. The purpose of anxiety is not to hurt you, but to alert you. It's there to help you when you think you're in danger. As such, it won't keep rising until you're completely out of control, and it won't go on forever.

Deliberately facing your fears instead of avoiding them or attempting to neutralize them is called *exposure*. Repeatedly engaging in exposure will actually decrease the frequency and intensity of your danger-related thoughts (and your peak level of anxiety) over time until eventually you are no longer afraid or anxious when faced with your feared situation. Exposure is therefore the most effective way of getting over fears in the long term. If you know how to drive a car, you went through the steps of exposure without even realizing it. You probably had many catastrophic thoughts and were quite anxious when you first got behind the wheel, but if you practiced driving often, it's likely that you had fewer danger-related thoughts and felt less and less anxious each time. Eventually, you became confident in your ability to drive a car and experienced little or no anxiety when driving. You also probably found that new driving challenges were difficult at first, but that practice diminished any fear or anxiety. For example, you probably felt anxious when you first drove on a major highway or had to parallel park, but over time and with repetition, it became easier.

How These Coping Mechanisms Work with Worry About Hypothetical Situations

You may be wondering how avoidance, neutralization, and exposure apply to worries about hypothetical situations, since these worries take place in your mind. With fears related to current real-life situations, such as a fear of elevators, most of the strategies associated with these three coping mechanisms (avoidance, neutralization, and exposure) are actions, or behaviors. The same strategies can be used with worries about hypothetical situations; however, they will be mental or cognitive in nature, as outlined in the sections that follow.

Avoidance of Worries

The two main strategies used to avoid worries about hypothetical situations are trying to block worry-related thoughts or engaging in distraction. If you've ever used either of these strategies, you probably found that they weren't very helpful. In fact, research has shown that trying to block or suppress thoughts doesn't work and can actually increase the frequency of the thoughts (Wegner 1994). This paradoxical increase in thoughts is called the *enhancement effect*, and it can occur with anything you try not to think about (Lavy and van den Hout 1990; Wenzlaff and Wegner 2000). As a short experiment, try to not think of an image of a white bear or the words "white bear" for sixty seconds. You can think about anything else you like—just don't think of a white bear…

If you tried that experiment, you probably found that you couldn't get white bears out of your mind. The same thing happens when you try not to think about worries about hypothetical situations: the more you try not to think about bad things happening, the more those thoughts seem to be stuck in your mind. As a result of that white bear thought experiment, you may also find yourself thinking of white bears from time to time over the next few days. This is because even when you're no longer trying to block a thought, it tends to continue to pop into your mind. This phenomenon is referred to as the *rebound effect*. The bottom line is that trying to block or suppress worries isn't just unhelpful; it can actually contribute to keeping your worries alive.

Distraction also isn't a very helpful strategy. If you put a great deal of effort into thinking about other things or doing something to take your mind off your worries, you might be successful while you're actively focusing your attention elsewhere. However, once you stop distracting yourself, your will worries return. This type of avoidance strategy is a bit like trying to push a beach ball underwater: it takes a lot of effort to keep the ball underwater, and once you let go of it, it immediately pops back out of the water.

Neutralizing Worries

You probably use several strategies to neutralize your worries and anxiety, and you might not even be aware that you're doing some of them. In terms of deliberate neutralizing strategies, many people try to reassure themselves by thinking things like *It probably won't happen* or trying to replace a negative thought with a positive thought. These strategies can temporarily make the feared situation seem less threatening and dampen your anxiety somewhat, but they maintain your fear in the same way that closing your eyes and pretending that you're elsewhere while on an elevator does: they fail to address your underlying fear. Moreover, when you don't fully experience your thoughts and associated anxiety without using these kinds of mental safety behaviors, you're likely to believe you'd be overwhelmed and unable to cope with your negative thoughts and anxiety if you didn't neutralize them in some way.

A strategy that you're probably using without being aware of it is *worry hopping*. To quash worry about one topic, you may shift to related but different topics. For example, if you worry, *What if there was an earthquake and I was seriously injured?* you might hop to other worries about the well-being of loved ones (*What if my children are at school during an earthquake? What if I can't reach them and they're hurt and scared?*), the condition of your home (*What if our house is severely damaged or destroyed? Where would we live?*), and financial issues (*What if insurance doesn't cover all the costs of repairs? We could lose all of our savings.*)

Each time you jump from one worry topic to another, you get a brief decrease in your anxiety about one worry, but your anxiety rises again with the next worry. Furthermore, shifting thoughts in this way is problematic because it prevents you from fully experiencing your thoughts about any single feared outcome. Before you have time to think about your feared outcome with one worry, you jump to another feared outcome, which interferes with new learning about the feared outcomes and the anxiety they provoke. In this way, worry hopping buffers you from your most catastrophic thoughts about a given worry and the anxiety that goes along with it, so you remain fearful and continue to worry excessively.

Exposure for Worries

As you can see, if you react to worries by trying to avoid them or trying to reduce their sting by using neutralization strategies, you'll actually be increasing the frequency of your worries in the long term. In other words, the fact that you try to not have these thoughts and the anxiety that goes with them is the main reason you keep having them. A more effective strategy is to use planned exposure to face your fears, in this case the feared outcomes you worry about in hypothetical situations.

Facing fears is a relatively clear-cut process when you're afraid of specific and concrete situations or objects, such as elevators, heights, or spiders. However, it's less straightforward when your fears involve thoughts about hypothetical situations that haven't yet happened. In this case, facing your fears head-on involves exposure to your feared outcome by writing a detailed description of your worst-case scenario (Goldman et al. 2007). This technique, called *written exposure*, allows you to experience the fear at the root of your worry as fully and vividly as possible in order to ultimately reduce your worries and anxiety over the long run.

Guidelines for Written Exposure

When facing any fear using exposure, there are two major rules. First, exposure requires repetition. To put yourself in a position to effectively reevaluate your fears and observe a consistent reduction in anxiety, you need to experience your feared thought or situation multiple times. This repetition allows you to consider the situation within a broad context, which will ultimately help you think about it differently and have little to no anxiety. Therefore, you need to conduct written exposure multiple times in order to fully benefit from it. We usually recommend completing written exposure three to five times a week for two to three weeks—the more often, the better.

Second, exposure must be prolonged. That is, you need to stay with a feared scenario long enough that you can come at it from different angles and develop a more flexible way of thinking about it. A common mistake many people make when doing exposure is to stay in a feared situation for only a few minutes, which is essentially the same as worry hopping: you have just enough time to begin to think about your feared outcome and become anxious before you exit the situation, and therefore don't get a chance to learn to think differently about the situation and see your anxiety start to drop. Leaving exposure early can also inadvertently mimic avoidance. Unfortunately, if you stop when your thoughts are at their most rigid and catastrophic and your anxiety is very high, you don't get any of the benefits of exposure, even though you were brave enough to face your fears. So plan on spending approximately thirty minutes completing each exposure session. That will give you enough time to fully and vividly imagine the feared outcome and hopefully to see your anxiety rise and fall within the session.

Because written exposure involves fully and repeatedly experiencing the anxiety associated with your worries, it's crucial to refrain from all strategies that involve any form of avoidance or neutralization. This will ensure that your scenario fully represents what you fear and is as anxiety provoking as possible. The following guidelines can help you with this.

Write in the First Person and the Present Tense

Thoughts about a hypothetical situation provoke anxiety when you imagine the situation happening to you *right now*. For this reason, write your scenario in the first person and the present tense to make the situation feel real. For example, if one of your worries involves being fired from work, you might write, "My boss looks at me with contempt and tells me that I'm fired effective immediately. I feel shame and embarrassment when I look over and see that all my coworkers heard him." Because it's in the present tense, the scenario feels more real than if it were written in the future tense: "My boss will look at me with contempt, and he'll tell me that I'm fired. What if my coworkers hear him? I would be so ashamed and embarrassed." You're also more likely to see yourself in the situation when you write from the first-person perspective, using "I," "me," and "my," rather than describing the scene like an outsider ("Her boss looks at her with contempt and tells her she's fired…"), which can distance you from both the situation and the anxiety it causes.

Include Information from Your Senses

When writing your scenario, make it as vivid as possible so you can mentally picture what you've written about, seeing it in your head. The best way to do this is to include information from as many of your senses as you can (sight, sound, touch, smell, and taste). If you think about your strongest and most powerful memories, they probably often involve some of your senses: the smell of food cooking, a song playing in the background, seeing the expression on a loved one's face, and so on. Because our senses have such a big impact on our emotional experience, you're more likely to clearly imagine your feared scenario when you include sensory information. For example, if your fear involves becoming seriously ill and being hospitalized, you might write about the smell of disinfectant in the hospital, the feel of an IV attached to your arm, or the sound of the doctor's voice.

Focus on the Worst-Case Scenario

It's important that your description capture what you most fear and that it be as anxiety provoking as possible, so you need to zero in on your worst-case scenario. For example, if you worry about natural disasters like hurricanes, tornadoes, or earthquakes, your worst-case scenario might involve your home being destroyed, being separated from loved ones with no way to find out whether they're okay, or being seriously injured yourself. If you find yourself resisting the idea of writing these thoughts because they're upsetting, remember that they are exactly the types of worries that have already been spinning in your head for weeks, months, or years, probably causing significant anxiety in the process. So getting upset by these thoughts is something you've already experienced repeatedly; now you'll simply be experiencing that deliberately as a tool for freeing yourself from worry, anxiety, and distress.

Make Sure Your Scenario Is Realistic

Although your scenario should describe your worst fear, it should also be believable. So don't write a scenario that you think could never happen; this would actually reduce your anxiety during exposure. For example, if you worry about being fired, your worst-case scenario might involve being unemployed, being unable to afford your home, and having to rely on friends or family members. If you don't think you'd end up homeless and living on the street, don't write about that.

Understanding the Goals of Exposure

By now you might be finding the idea of conducting written exposure very scary. Maybe you don't even want to try it. This would be understandable, since you've probably been devoting a lot of effort to not thinking these thoughts for years. As a result, focusing on your worst fears might seem like a bad idea. So before you start doing written exposure, it's important to understand the goals of exposure, as well as what exposure doesn't aim to do.

You might be concerned that one of the goals of exposure is to reduce your fear of a negative situation should it actually occur—to not care if bad things happen. This isn't the case. For example, if one of your worries involves a loved one being seriously injured or killed in an accident, the goal of exposure is not to help you feel nothing if this should ever happen. If a loved one were injured or killed, this would obviously be a terrible and distressing situation. However, there are many negative things that *could* happen in life, and the fact that they could happen doesn't mean they *will* happen. Having them at the front of your mind on a daily basis is both unhelpful and upsetting. A primary goal of exposure is to allow worries about hypothetical situations to remain in the back of your mind, where they belong. If you find yourself resisting written exposure, remind yourself that you've chosen to work with this book so you won't spend your days thinking about all the negative things that could happen. This will open the door to enjoying your life in the moment.

EXERCISE 10.2: Practicing Written Exposure

Now that you have some guidelines for conducting written exposure, you can begin to apply it to one of your own worries about a hypothetical situation. Pick one of the worries you listed earlier in this chapter, choosing something you worry about frequently and find particularly anxiety provoking. With written exposure, it's usually best to start with the most distressing worry. Beyond that, here are a few specific guidelines:

- **Practice frequently and for sufficient duration.** Practice written exposure three to five times a week. Plan on writing continuously at a moderate pace for thirty minutes each time.

205

- **Set a scheduled time for exposure.** Because written exposure involves staying focused on your worst-case scenario for an extended period of time, it's a good idea to set up some private time, when you won't be interrupted, to do it.

- **Don't worry about spelling or grammar.** Focus on writing the first thing that comes to mind. Your writing style while doing this exercise doesn't matter.

- **Stick to the same worry topic.** Although we encourage you to go deeper into your worst-case scenario each time you conduct written exposure, be sure to write about the same topic each time.

- **Include your emotional reactions in your scenario.** Don't forget to include your feelings in the description of your worst-case scenario, such as feeling overwhelmed, terrified, confused, or embarrassed.

When conducting written exposure, it's helpful to record your thoughts and anxiety in order to see your progress. You can use the Exposure Summary Form that follows (available for download at http://www.newharbinger.com/31519) at each exposure session.

Keeping these guidelines in mind, you're ready to begin. You can write your first description of your worst-case scenario anytime. You may wish to keep a separate notebook or electronic file for this purpose.

Remember that you can expect to feel anxious at the beginning of a written exposure session. However, over the course of the session your anxiety level should start to drop, and as you do more sessions, even your initial anxiety will be lower. You can stop practicing written exposure when describing your worst-case scenario causes little to no anxiety throughout an entire session, reflecting that you've adopted new thoughts about the scenario.

EXPOSURE SUMMARY FORM

Theme of scenario: _____

To Complete Before Exposure

Time started: _____

Current level of anxiety about your worst-case scenario (0 to 10): _____

To Complete After Exposure

Time ended: _____

Current level of anxiety about your worst-case scenario (0 to 10): _____

Probability that your worst-case scenario will actually happen (0 to 100 percent): _____?

How catastrophic it would it be if your worst-case scenario actually happened (0 to 100 percent): _____

The extent to which you'd be able to deal with your worst-case scenario if it actually happened (0 to 100 percent): _____

Troubleshooting Written Exposure

Conducting written exposure can be tricky. In the sections that follow, we address some common concerns and challenges that you might experience and provide suggestions on how to deal with them.

Difficulties Getting Started

In our clinical practice, we've found that some people have a hard time getting started with written exposure. This isn't surprising, because facing your worst fears, even in written form, can be very distressing. You might find that you've been putting off this exercise, perhaps with excuses like *I'm really busy right now. I think I should wait a few weeks until I have more time to spend on exposure.* Unfortunately, there will never be a perfect time to do written exposure. No one enjoys thinking about feared negative outcomes or feeling anxious. Ultimately, it's up to you to decide whether your worries about hypothetical situations are problematic enough that you want to start dealing with them head-on, rather than with your current coping strategies. If you think exposure would be helpful, work written exposure into your schedule, then follow through with it no matter how you feel at the time. Keep in mind that the hardest part of starting any new task is the first few steps; it will get easier with time and practice.

Another roadblock to getting started with exposure can be a lingering concern that written exposure won't actually be helpful. Some of our clients have feared that they're tempting fate by thinking about their worst fears, or believe that it's better to focus on positive thoughts, rather than thinking about worst-case scenarios. We have two responses. First, simply thinking about negative events doesn't make them happen. Remember that you've probably been worrying about potential problems for years; if thinking about them could make them occur, they would already have happened. Second, you've probably already tried to replace worries with positive thoughts, and given that you're reading this book, it's unlikely that this strategy was successful. If it were possible to simply replace one thought with another, you probably would already have done so. Once again, it's up to you to decide whether it's worthwhile to you to experience the short-term distress of focusing intensively on feared outcomes in order to obtain the long-term gain of moving these worries to the back of your mind.

Not Experiencing Anxiety

Some people report that they don't experience anxiety when conducting written exposure. If this is the case for you, you'll need to figure out why you aren't experiencing anxiety in order to address it. There can be several reasons. One is using neutralization strategies while writing. Without realizing it, some people diminish the intensity of what they're writing by softening the scenario. For example, if you're writing about losing your job, you might write "My coworkers offer me sympathy and tell me that I'll easily find another job" or "My boss apologizes and tells me that he doesn't want to fire me, but that he has no choice." You might also unintentionally include qualifying language, such as "I know that this wouldn't happen" or "Eventually I realize that everything will be fine." These types of statements make the scenario less threatening, which might account for an absence of anxiety during exposure. We recommend that you read through your written exposure exercises to determine whether you've been using neutralizing language. If so, try to stay focused on your worst-case scenario in future sessions.

Another potential reason for not experiencing anxiety during exposure is having distractions in your environment that prevent you from fully experiencing fear of your scenario. This can include having music or the television playing in the background or thinking about other things while writing your scenario. Remember that the goal of exposure is to focus on your feared outcome as if it were happening in the moment. To that end, remove as many distractions as you can so you can focus your attention on the exercise.

It's also possible that you aren't experiencing anxiety during written exposure because your fear is no longer severe enough to elicit anxiety. Sometimes simply writing down a feared scenario allows you to see it as just that: a description of a scenario that isn't very likely and may never happen. Because worry typically involves hopping from one topic to another, you might not have had a good opportunity to see a vivid and complete picture of a particular worry until you wrote out a feared scenario. Although we encourage you to conduct exposure for two to three weeks, you may find that your fear and anxiety are reduced after just a few exposure sessions. In that case, your difficulty experiencing anxiety during exposure might be because you overcame your fear more quickly than expected. If so, we recommend that you conduct a couple more exposure sessions to ensure that your scenario continues to produce no anxiety before discontinuing the exercise.

Increase in Worry and Anxiety After Exposure

Some of our clients have reported that their anxiety and worry increased after a few exposure sessions. If this happens to you, you might think written exposure only makes things worse, or that you're back to square one. In fact, experiencing an initial increase in anxiety and worry isn't that uncommon, and given that you're focusing on your worst fears, it isn't entirely surprising. Bear in mind that this increase in distress is only temporary. With repeated practice, your worry and anxiety will eventually decrease. As such, we strongly recommend not stopping written exposure until your anxiety throughout a session is consistently low. Given the time and effort this strategy requires, you don't want to discontinue the practice before you fully benefit from it.

Taking Perspective on Your Worries

Once you complete written exposure for a particular worry, it's likely that both your anxiety and the frequency of your worry will be greatly diminished. In addition, that particular feared outcome might seem less probable or catastrophic, or you might feel more confident in your ability to manage the situation should it occur. For example, if your worry involved being fired from your job, you may come to think that although this would be very negative, you could probably find a new job if you had to. Or if your worry is about losing a loved one in an accident, you might come to see this as a terrible thing if it happened, but not something you need to think about every day, given that there's little chance it will actually occur. In this case, you might find that you can more easily let this worry go, freeing you to think about other things.

Why would you look at your worries in a new way after completing written exposure? Focusing on your worst-case scenario allows you to objectively evaluate the entire situation, including how likely it is to happen, how bad it would actually be, and how you'd cope if it did occur. Having this complete picture allows you to gather information about how dangerous the situation actually is—information you couldn't access when you were trying to avoid or neutralize that particular worry. In this way, focusing on your feared outcome repeatedly allows you to reevaluate the situation as significantly less threatening, which reduces your worry.

You might be wondering whether you need to conduct written exposure for every remaining worry you have about hypothetical situations. Fortunately this isn't the case. Most people's worries about hypothetical situations involve just one or two underlying fears, such as a fear of being alone and isolated, of being unable to care for themselves, or of witnessing the pain and suffering of loved ones. One such fear can underlie several different worry topics, so once you address that fear, all worries related to it will be reduced, not just the one you targeted with exposure. For example, if your fear is being unable to care for yourself, you might worry about the end of a relationship, health problems as you get older, or losing your job. When you conduct written exposure for one of these worries, you'll probably notice that they all diminish in frequency.

Fitting Written Exposure into Your Coping Toolbox

Written exposure, like problem solving, is an approach you can use if you find that you have some remaining worries that continue to be excessive and chronic. However, given all the work that you've done in this book so far, you might find that this strategy isn't necessary for you. In fact, it's common for people to discover that once they start writing down a detailed description of their worry, they quickly gain perspective on the situation and feel less concerned about it.

You might also find that when you start to write down a worry, you notice that there are actually a number of safety behaviors you use to cope with it. For example, if you're worried about the health of your parents, you might monitor what they eat, ask them regularly how often they exercise, or seek information online about any symptoms you think you've observed. Targeting these safety behaviors through a behavioral experiment might be a more efficient strategy in this case. Whether or not you feel that you need to complete written exposure again for a particular concern, you can view it as yet another tool in your toolbox for the long-term management of your worries.

CHAPTER 11

Building on Gains: Managing Worries over Time

At this point in the book, you've learned a number of strategies for better understanding and managing your worry, and hopefully you've begun to see some positive changes in your life. Perhaps you find that you're more willing to try new things, or that you worry less in situations that were anxiety provoking for you in the past. It's important to recognize and celebrate your gains. Also, regardless of how much progress you've made so far, it's crucial to maintain and build upon your gains well into the future. To that end, this chapter focuses on how to manage your worries in the long term.

Placing Mental Health in Context

Before we discuss how to maintain the gains you've derived from the strategies in this workbook, we'd like you to take a step back and consider what you've learned within the broader context of mental health. Mental health is very similar to other aspects of health, such as dental and physical health, even though our culture doesn't generally treat it that way. When you think about taking care of your teeth or your body, you probably already know that this requires some effort on your part. If you want to have healthy teeth, you know that you need to brush and floss every day, be careful to not eat too many sweets, and go to the dentist for regular checkups. If you didn't do any of these things, you'd probably experience a lot of dental problems over time.

Mental health, which essentially involves feeling comfortable in your own skin and being able to manage adversity, is similar. If you don't devote any effort to taking care of your own well-being and managing the difficulties that come up in daily life, you can expect to feel worse over time. Yet for some reason, our society tends to view mental health as something that should take care of itself—that you shouldn't have to work at being a generally happy and content person. Of course, this isn't true. Care and maintenance of your mental health requires the same kind of effort you put into the care of your body. So maintaining the benefits you've received from the strategies in this workbook—and hopefully improving upon them over time—will require some consistent effort on your part.

The Journey Ahead

Mastering your worry management skills is a bit like learning how to play the piano. You might decide to take some lessons with a piano teacher, who would teach you the basics of how to play and encourage you to practice what you've learned each week before teaching you something new. At the end of your course of instruction, you probably wouldn't be an excellent pianist, but you would have some good basic knowledge of how to play. Where you go from there is up to you. If you don't keep practicing and trying new things on the piano, your newly acquired skills will start to fade. If you want to remember what you learned, and even improve your abilities, you need to keep practicing.

CBT skills function in the same way. At this point in the book, it's likely that you've made some headway in reducing your GAD symptoms. However, you probably aren't entirely free of excessive worry, especially if you've only had a couple of months of practice with thinking and behaving differently in triggering situations. Depending upon how much time you've spent working on each of the chapters, you have greater or lesser expertise with the various strategies for reducing worry presented in this book. But if you close this workbook now and quit practicing the skills you've acquired, over time your worries and safety behaviors are likely to start creeping back into your life. For this reason, you need to have a plan for how you'll keep using your worry management skills over the long run. In essence, as you near the end of this workbook you're arriving at the beginning of a new journey—one that can lead not only to a life without excessive worry, but also to a life with good overall mental health.

Maintenance Skills

Skills for maintaining your gains can be divided into two types: those that involve caring for your mental health in general, and those that specifically address your worries. General mental health strategies are helpful for everyone, regardless of whether they've struggled with significant mood or anxiety problems at some point in life. They are preventative strategies, just like regularly brushing your teeth—in this case designed to aid you in coping with the difficulties that we all face in daily life. In contrast, worry-specific strategies are designed to help you to maintain and build upon the progress you've made in reducing excessive worry.

Practicing Self-Care

Learning to practice self-care is a general mental health strategy that can include anything you do that's pleasant, relaxing, or enjoyable. What constitutes good self-care depends on the person. Some people enjoy going to the gym or going for a walk, others prefer setting aside time to read a book or take a leisurely bath, and yet others like to get together with friends or watch a favorite show on television.

Engaging in regular self-care is an excellent buffer against the daily stressors of life because it allows you to calm down and generally feel more mentally able to cope with adversity. Unfortunately, as the number of stressful events increases, people tend to reduce the amount of time they devote to self-care activities. For example, perhaps you like to cook dinner for your family two or three times a week because it's pleasant for you and allows you to spend time with family members discussing events of the day. However, if you find yourself behind on work deadlines, you might skip making dinner for a few weeks and eat take-out at your desk instead. The problem with this is that falling behind on deadlines is stressful, but instead of engaging in activities that can offset that stress (cooking dinner), you've removed that self-care activity from your schedule.

Think of your capacity for stress as an empty cup. As life throws difficulties your way (getting a flat tire, misplacing your keys, having a bad night's sleep after the smoke alarm went off during the night), your cup starts to gradually fill. When you regularly engage in self-care, you're taking a spoon and emptying out the cup a bit, preventing it from overflowing. In the absence of that slow and steady stress reduction, you can become overwhelmed by stress and easily frazzled by minor events (for example, getting extremely angry when you hit too many red lights on the way home).

Self-care activities are therefore not just pleasant events; they're extremely important for long-term management of stress and anxiety. This is particularly the case when you're struggling with GAD, since it will be more challenging to follow through on worry management techniques if you're overwhelmed by day-to-day stressors.

Making Time for Self-Care

Many of our clients can identify numerous self-care activities they'd enjoy and even report that they've been meaning to do them for a while but never found the time. Yet we all take time for the things we consider important. So remember, self-care is an essential component of managing your overall mental health. As such, you need to identify self-care activities you can engage in during the week and then schedule them, just as you'd schedule an appointment with the dentist. You can do some self-care strategies on a weekly or daily basis, such as going for a walk every day or having a weekly date night with your significant other. Other activities can be considered special events or rewards that you might engage in on occasion, such as going to a concert or a movie with friends or spending a day at the spa.

It's a good idea to plan a few self-care activities each week. Of course, sometimes you need to be flexible. For example, you might have less free time available for self-care if you have a child who's sick with the flu or if you have extra work to do at school or at your job. Still, even when you have less time to devote to yourself, be sure to continue to engage in some form of self-care. Even small amounts of time can be helpful, such as allowing yourself twenty minutes to read the newspaper or a magazine while drinking a cup of tea.

EXERCISE 11.1: Identifying and Scheduling Self-Care Activities

Because of the importance of self-care activities for good mental health, we recommend that you keep a list of various activities that you find pleasant, enjoyable, or relaxing. Ideally, you should have a mix of indoor and outdoor activities so there's always something that you have the option of doing regardless of the weather (you might not go for a walk on a cold or rainy day) or the time of day (you might not go out for coffee with friends late at night). Here are some categories of self-care activities you might consider, along with examples in case that's helpful. Try to write down activities in as many categories as possible. We encourage you to prioritize and schedule self-care activities. To facilitate making this an ongoing process, we've provided downloadable versions of the following worksheets at http://www.newharbinger.com/31519.

Physical activities (going to the gym; going for a walk, a jog, or a hike; or playing tennis, golf, hockey, or any other team or group sport)

Activities you would enjoy: _____

_____

_____

Social activities (going out to lunch or dinner with a friend; spending time with your significant other or children; or engaging in a recreational activity with friends, such as shopping, seeing a movie, or being a tourist in your hometown and visiting local museums and attractions)

Activities you would enjoy: _____

_____

_____

Pampering activities (spending time at a spa; getting a manicure, a facial, or a massage; taking a long relaxing bath; making your favorite treat at home; taking time to read a book; or watching a favorite film or television show)

Activities you would enjoy: _____

_____

_____

Other activities (taking your dog for a walk; doing arts and crafts; or taking a class that interests you, such as an art class, dance lessons, or a cooking or wine class)

Activities you would enjoy: _____

_____

_____

Now that you have a list of activities you might like to engage in for self-care, schedule at least two activities per week. If there's an activity that you'd like to do on a weekly basis, find a specific time to do so. For example, if you'd like to go to the gym twice a week before work, pick a specific day and time, such as Mondays and Wednesdays at 7:30 a.m. To get started, use the following form to record the two activities you plan to engage in over the next week, as well as the date and time you'll do them. If an activity requires a bit more planning, list the steps to increase the chances that you'll follow through. Once the scheduled time has passed, also record whether you actually did the activity.

SAMPLE SELF-CARE ACTIVITIES FOR THE WEEK

Activity 1: *Go to a movie with some friends.*

Date and time: *Friday evening*

Any preparations needed? *Check to see which movies are playing, and ask friends to see who would like to come along.*

Activity 2: *Watch a football game.*

Date and time: *Sunday at 1 p.m.*

Any preparations needed? *Pick up some snacks to eat while watching the game.*

SELF-CARE ACTIVITIES FOR THE WEEK

Activity 1: _____

Date and time: _____

Any preparations needed? _____

_____

_____

Completed? Yes _____   No _____

Activity 2: _____

Date and time: _____

Any preparations needed? _____

_____

_____

Completed? Yes _____   No _____

Becoming Your Own Therapist

In terms of specific worry-management skills, one of the most important ways to ensure that you maintain and strengthen your gains is to consistently set aside a weekly time to plan the exercises you'll practice over the next week. We call this "becoming your own therapist." As mentioned in the introduction, one of the benefits of seeing a therapist is accountability. A CBT therapist will help you develop exercises to practice every week and then review those exercises with you in session. Knowing that someone will be asking you what you did and how it went often provides good motivation to complete the exercises.

Becoming your own therapist means taking on that role yourself, devising your own exercises, reviewing how they went, and then assigning yourself new exercises. In order to follow through on this, you need to make an appointment with yourself, just like making an appointment with a therapist. You might go to a coffee shop for an hour, or simply schedule that time at home, choosing a time when you're unlikely to be interrupted (this might mean turning off your cell phone!). In the sections that follow, we'll outline a few helpful topics to review during your session with yourself.

WEEKLY CHECK-IN

As a first step, you might want to check in with yourself to see how your week was: Did you worry a lot? If so, what did you worry about? Were there any particular stressors that might account for the worry? For example, you might find that you worry more about school during exams, or about the state of your house when you have family visiting.

REVIEW OF EXERCISES

Your session might also include a review of the exercises you've been working on. Writing down your accomplishments is an important part of long-term maintenance, allowing you to see whether you've continued to make improvements. For example, you may have conducted some behavioral experiments that would have been much too difficult for you a few weeks before. This review can also help you identify areas that are still very challenging for you and give you ideas for new experiments to try.

MASTERED SKILLS AND SKILLS TO MASTER

We offered a number of strategies in this workbook, and how comfortable you are with each one probably differs. During your appointment with yourself, you might want to briefly review all of these strategies to determine which you feel comfortable with (mastered skills) and which you could use more practice with (skills yet to be mastered). The skills that have been useful for reducing your worry are the most important ones to practice if you want to continue worrying less. Here's a list of the strategies you've learned so far in this book:

- **Self-monitoring.** As a rule, you can't rely on your memory if you want to detect a pattern in your thoughts, behaviors, or emotions. Therefore, self-monitoring is an invaluable tool anytime you begin to notice that you're generally more worried and anxious. You can use self-monitoring to track your worries, safety behaviors, triggering situations, anxiety levels, and types of worry. If you decide to engage in self-monitoring, it's a good idea to do so for at least a week to give you enough time to notice any problematic patterns.

- **Distinguishing worry types.** If you're monitoring your worries, it can be helpful to note whether your worries are predominantly about current problems, hypothetical situations, or both. This will help you determine your next step in dealing with the problem.

- **Identifying and challenging your beliefs about the usefulness of worry.** When you believe a particular worry is beneficial, you're less likely to want to address it. Recognizing any positive beliefs about worry that you hold and testing those beliefs by challenging your thoughts and conducting behavioral experiments is a helpful tool when you find that it's difficult to let go of certain worries.

- **Setting goals for a life without worry.** Remember that you decided to learn the strategies in this book so you could ultimately feel happier and more content in your life. Reducing your worries is a significant component of that goal, but it's also important to consider the next steps in your life. As a part of your session with yourself, it's a good idea to revisit your goals for yourself on occasion and to decide whether you need to add new goals or change old ones.

- **Recognizing your GAD safety behaviors.** Knowing the behaviors you typically engage in to try to either reduce or avoid uncertainty can help you spot old patterns early on if they start to creep up.

- **Conducting behavioral experiments to challenge negative beliefs about uncertainty.** This is one of the most important tools in managing excessive worry in the long term. As much as possible, try to weave experiments into your daily life so they eventually become new habits.

- **Challenging negative problem orientation.** This is particularly helpful if you find that you're starting to worry more about current problems but putting off dealing with them. Remember that your beliefs about problems and problem solving are a more powerful determining factor in what you'll do when faced with a problem than your actual problem-solving skills are.

- **Effective problem solving.** Using your problem-solving skills effectively can not only help you deal with difficult situations in life, but also increase your confidence in the face of adversity and provide a direct contrast between actively dealing with life's problems and worrying about them.

- **Written exposure.** This strategy for coping with worries about hypothetical situations can be emotionally challenging. However, in order to get over your fears, you sometimes have to face them head-on.

EXERCISE 11.2: Conducting a Session with Yourself

Because any success you've had in reducing your worry and anxiety is probably relatively recent, it's a good idea to initially have a weekly session with yourself. Try to set aside an hour in your weekly schedule, along with a specific time and place for the session. To assist you in becoming your own therapist, you can use the following worksheet (available for download at http://www.newharbinger.com/31519) to make notes and move through the suggested agenda. Feel free to add or substitute any questions that you think would be helpful. You can definitely add or remove items from your agenda, since you are your own therapist! If you do want to cover different topics or questions, be sure to keep a written record of your sessions either in a notebook or electronically.

SESSION AGENDA

Weekly Check-In

How anxious were you overall this week on a scale of 0 to 10? _____

On average, how much did you worry this week (percent of your waking day)? _____

What are some of the topics you worried about?

_____

_____

_____

Were some of your worries excessive or uncontrollable? If so, which ones?

_____

_____

Were there any stressors this week that might account for your worry? If so, what was happening?

_____

_____

_____

If you've had more stress than usual, how did you deal with it? Did you use any additional self-care strategies?

_____

_____

_____

Did you experience any of the following symptoms this week? If so, how severe were they on a scale of 0 to 10?

Feeling restless, keyed up, or on edge _____

Being easily fatigued _____

Difficulty concentrating or mind going blank _____

Irritability _____

Muscle tension _____

Sleep disturbances _____

Did you catch yourself engaging in any GAD-related safety behaviors? If so, which ones?

_____

_____

_____

Overall, do you feel that your worry and anxiety were better or worse this week compared to recent weeks?

_____

Exercise Review

Did you practice any exercises this week? If so, what did you do?

_____

_____

_____

Were any exercises easier than expected? If so, is there a way to make new exercises more challenging?

_____

_____

_____

Were any exercises harder than expected? Was there an exercise you wanted to do but didn't because it seemed too difficult? If so, is there a way to make new exercises slightly less challenging and more doable?

_____

_____

_____

Skills Review

Looking at all your worry management skills, do you think you could use extra practice with any of them? If so, which ones, and what could you do?

_____

_____

_____

Setting Exercises for the Upcoming Week

Keeping in mind the exercises you did last week and any skills you might need to work on, what exercises can you do over the coming week? If possible, try to do two or three exercises weekly.

Exercise 1: _____

Exercise 2: _____

Exercise 3: _____

Date and time for next session: _____

The Ongoing Process of Maintaining Gains

As mentioned at the beginning of this chapter, managing your worries, and your overall mental health, is a lifelong process. Although we encourage you to have weekly sessions with yourself to ensure that you regularly practice your new skills, as you become more confident you can start scheduling your sessions once every two weeks, then once a month, and eventually every four to six months. At that point, consider your sessions with yourself as checkups—something you do a couple of times per year even if everything is going well. These sessions will give you an opportunity to reflect on how you're doing and to praise yourself for all of the hard work you've done.

CHAPTER 12

Bumps in the Road: Coping with Lapses and Relapses

When it comes to managing worry and anxiety, progress seldom moves in a straight line. Almost everyone experiences ups and downs. You might find that sometimes you worry more than usual, and other times you worry less. This is absolutely normal. However, on occasion you might find that you've had a significant downturn in progress. This can be frustrating and demoralizing, and you might be unsure what to do to get back on track. The problem is complicated by the fact that all dips in progress are not created equal. They can differ depending on cause and severity, and in the approach most appropriate for turning the situation around. This chapter focuses on managing these bumps in the road: how to recognize them, or even prevent them before they happen, and what to do when you realize that you're experiencing a downturn in your progress.

Normal vs. Problematic Lapses

The first step in being prepared to cope with problematic lapses is to understand that increases in anxiety and worry can be a normal experience and to recognize when this is the case. Everyone worries or feels anxiety sometimes. Simply having an increase in these experiences doesn't necessarily mean you aren't coping well. In general, you can view an increase in anxiety and worry in one of two ways: as a normal response to an extreme situation, or as an extreme response to a normal situation. In the first case, the problem isn't actually your anxiety or worry, but the situation that initially caused it. In other words, anyone who was in your shoes would probably have a similar reaction. For example, if you need surgery due to an illness, you'll probably be quite anxious about both the surgery and your health. This reaction can be considered normal and appropriate because this situation would probably be a stressful one for most people.

In contrast, if you find that you're worrying a great deal about minor stressors, similar to how much you worried before starting this workbook, this would probably indicate a more problematic lapse. For example, if situations like going to a new restaurant or choosing a present for someone's birthday were to cause you significant anxiety and worry, this would be considered an extreme reaction to a normal situation—a reaction more severe than the situation warrants.

Understanding Normal Lapses

With respect to normal lapses, there are two situations in which most people tend to experience more anxiety and worry: when experiencing negative moods and during times of stress.

THE IMPACT OF NEGATIVE MOODS

When you're feeling down or in a bad mood, you're more likely to react negatively to day-to-day situations because your mood can color your view of the world. Bad situations can seem worse than they are, and challenges can seem more overwhelming. Fortunately, the way you look at and react to situations can change once your mood improves. You may have noticed for yourself that things can look very different once you get over a negative mood. For example, say you're invited to go camping with a group of friends and you're feeling down. You're likely to decline the invitation, preferring to stay home alone rather than to put forth all the effort involved in preparing to go camping and socializing with others. However, if your mood were better later in the day, you might think very differently about the idea of going camping. Spending time with friends might sound like fun, and you might be excited about sitting around a campfire and chatting with everyone.

It's the same with increases in anxiety and worry that are due to a negative mood. Daily life situations can appear more threatening when you're feeling down or upset, which can make you more likely to react with anxiety and worry. This happens to everyone from time to time. Once your negative feelings pass, you might evaluate the same situations differently.

THE IMPACT OF STRESSFUL LIFE EVENTS

Day-to-day stressors can also increase most people's anxiety. Even positive events, such as getting married, moving to a new home, or being promoted at work, can be stressful. Although stress typically arises due to major changes in a person's daily life, it can also involve several minor changes or inconveniences that accrue over time. Nuisances such as forgetting your cell phone at home, coming back from a trip and experiencing jet lag, or not having an umbrella when it suddenly starts to rain are all relatively minor problems. However, if you experience all of them at around the same time, it can be extremely stressful. Whether you're experiencing a single significant stressful event or multiple smaller problems, stress can increase your anxiety level, making you more prone to worry about minor things you wouldn't have under less stressful circumstances.

Coping with Normal Lapses

Because mood and stress level can influence anxiety and worry, it's a good idea to consider these factors if you notice that you're more worried or anxious than usual. This can allow you to place your increased distress in context and shift the focus away from you and toward whatever is leading to your stress or negative mood.

So ask yourself whether there's been a significant change in your mood or an increase in stress that might account for your heightened worry and anxiety. In particular, ask yourself whether your current situation would be considered upsetting or stressful to most anyone. Would someone who doesn't have GAD feel more anxious and worried if in your shoes? Taking the time to identify whether the problem is the situation, rather than your reaction to it, allows you to focus on the problem at hand rather than blaming yourself for how you're feeling. Specifically, you can focus on dealing with the problematic situation if possible, or on improving your mood or engaging in stress-reducing activities.

Problematic Lapses

Sometimes increases in anxiety and worry are more problematic and reflect a gradual backslide into old ways of thinking and behaving. If you have a problematic lapse, you'll probably notice that you start using some of the safety behaviors you identified and worked on in earlier chapters. For example, you might notice that you've started double-checking some of your texts or e-mails before sending them, or that you're procrastinating a bit more before making decisions. In this case, the increase in your anxiety and worry is probably due to a gradual return of old habits and starting to view unpredictable, novel, or ambiguous situations as threatening again.

Lapses vs. Relapses

Regardless of whether a lapse is a normal reaction to an extreme situation or an extreme reaction to a normal situation, it isn't necessarily a relapse. A lapse is a short-term increase in symptoms, whereas a relapse is a more lengthy return to how you were functioning before you started working on your anxiety and worry. Relapses usually occur as a reaction to a lapse, because how you interpret a dip in your progress influences what you'll do next. If you view a lapse as a failure or a sign that you're back to square one, you're more likely to feel discouraged and decide to give up on trying to manage your anxiety and worry. If, on the other hand, you view a lapse as a normal part of overall progress, then you're more likely to address it quickly and continue moving forward. It's important to remember that whether you're experiencing a lapse or a relapse, you can turn the situation around and start building on your progress again. However, it's often easier to do so when you're experiencing a lapse.

Managing Lapses

The best way to feel confident in your ability to manage any kind of dip in progress is to have strategies to deal with difficulties at all stages. So in the sections that follow, we'll help you identify early warning signs of having a lapse, the early stages of a lapse, and when a lapse has progressed to a relapse. We will also offer skills you can use at each stage.

Early Warning Signs

In order to catch lapses early, it's a good idea to identify early warning signs that alert you that your anxiety and worry are increasing. This can include general signs common to most people, as well as those that are specific to you. General warning signs often involve feeling run-down, fatigued, or irritated, or having difficulty concentrating. For example, you might become easily irritated by minor inconveniences that wouldn't normally bother you, like someone being five minutes late to meet you. Or you might find that you have to reread an email or newspaper article several times in order to get the point. None of these warning signs guarantees that you'll have an increase in anxiety and worry. However, feeling physically taxed can make you more vulnerable.

Early warning signs that are specific to you involve any thoughts or behaviors that serve as a signal that you might be falling back into some of your old habits. This can include engaging in more frequent safety behaviors, like double-checking, excessively seeking information or reassurance, or procrastinating. Other possibilities for personal warning signs include engaging in fewer self-care activities, getting into arguments with loved ones, or noticing that you seem to be worrying a bit more about issues you had largely stopped worrying about. Because everyone is different, there are countless other early warning signs. In the following exercise, we'll provide more examples to help you see the possibilities. The point is, it's worthwhile to know your warning signs, because this can be a powerful tool that allows you to address potential lapses before they even begin.

EXERCISE 12.1: Identifying Your Early Warning Signs

This exercise is designed to help you identify your own early warning signs. We present them in various categories. When considering each category, take some time to think about what lets you know that you aren't doing as well as you'd like. (Because your warning signs may change over time, or you may identify new ones, we've provided a downloadable version of this worksheet at http://www.newharbinger.com/31519.)

Feeling run-down (This can include feeling irritable or fatigued or having difficulty with concentration.)

_____

_____

Changes in sleep (This can include difficulty sleeping, taking more naps or fewer ones, or going to bed or getting up earlier or later than usual.)

_____

_____

Safety behaviors (This includes any uncertainty-related safety behaviors that you've used in the past and that you notice you're starting to use again.)

_____

_____

Engaging in less self-care (This can include changing or dropping any activities that you enjoy or find relaxing, such as making dinner at home, reading, going to the gym, playing sports with friends, or giving yourself a manicure.)

_____

_____

Changes at home (This can include not attending to housecleaning, not taking care of family finances, or not spending time with family members.)

_____

_____

Changes at work or school (This can include any changes in your work or study habits, your productivity, or interactions with colleagues or friends at work or school.)

_____

_____

Taking Action When You Notice Early Warning Signs

When you're able to recognize your warning signs early, you can take steps to address them right away, before anxiety and worry become a problem. This might involve making a conscious effort to reduce problematic behaviors or taking the time to engage in pleasant or relaxing activities you usually enjoy—in other words, self-care. For example, if one of your warning signs is not spending time with family and friends and you notice this happening, you might arrange a pleasant outing with them. Likewise, if not exercising is a warning sign for you and you notice that you haven't been going to the gym, you can take steps to fit exercise into your schedule.

These kinds of activities can be particularly helpful if your warning signs suggest that there's increased stress in your life, since it isn't always possible to change a difficult situation right away. If you're working under a deadline, for example, you might need to spend more time at work for a few days, so you'd have less time to go to the gym or allow yourself some downtime at home. In this case, it's a good idea to develop a concrete self-care plan you can follow once you've met your deadline, or to give yourself small self-care moments each day, such as taking a thirty-minute break from work to eat lunch, read, or go for a walk.

If your warning signs suggest that you've started using unhelpful old safety behaviors again, such as checking your phone repeatedly or asking for reassurance from others, you might choose to conduct a behavioral experiment to nip these behaviors in the bud.

Noticing warning signs, and then taking action once you've recognized them, can also be a part of a weekly or monthly session you have with yourself, as described in exercise 11.2. Because dealing with bumps in the road is a normal part of managing your overall mental health, identifying your early warning signs can serve as yet another strategy to help you build and improve upon your gains.

Early Lapses

If you've started to revert to old habits—for example engaging in more safety behaviors, or worrying more about daily life events—either because you noticed your early warning signs or because you're just feeling more anxious and distressed, then you're probably experiencing a lapse. As mentioned earlier, this is absolutely normal, although it is a good idea to start dealing with the lapse as quickly as possible in order to get back on track and return to maintaining and building upon your former gains. The following exercise will help you to cope with an early lapse as soon as you start to notice it.

EXERCISE 12.2: Making a Plan to Deal with Early Lapses

Because there are several different types of early warning signs, as well as different reasons why you might have started to experience an early lapse, it can be helpful to have a plan to get back on track no matter what the initial trigger was. This exercise will help you create a plan of action for addressing any kind of early lapse. (To download this worksheet for use with future lapses, visit http://www.newharbinger.com/31519.)

Identifying a Normal Lapse

Have you noticed a change in your mood recently? Yes _____   No _____

Has anything in particular been happening in your life that might account for your mood change? If so, what?

_____

_____

_____

Have there been any significant changes or stresses in your life? If so, what?

_____

_____

_____

Is your change in mood or increase in stress due to a current difficult life situation? In other words, does your increase in anxiety and worry seem appropriate given this situation?

Yes _____   No _____

If you're experiencing an increase in stress, is there something you can do to manage the stress? (For example, if the stress involves a significant increase in work demands, can you delegate some tasks to others or get a deadline extended to reduce your daily workload?) If so, what can you do?

_____

_____

_____

If there's nothing you can do at this time to manage the stressful situation, what self-care activities can you do to cope with the situation? (For example, perhaps you can go for a walk, watch a movie, take a yoga class, or meet with friends.)

_____

_____

_____

Coping with a Problematic Lapse

If your increase in anxiety and worry doesn't seem to be a normal reaction to stressful or difficult external events, answer the following questions.

Has there been a change in your daily self-care, including sleeping and eating regularly, taking some time for yourself, going to the gym, or spending time with your family?

Yes _____   No _____

If so, how can you address this? (For example, perhaps you can plan some social outings, make sure to take thirty minutes each workday to have lunch, or go to bed at approximately the same time each evening.)

_____

_____

_____

If you identified an increase in safety behaviors as an early warning sign, are there any behavioral experiments you can do? (For example, you could refrain from checking your cell phone more than once during the day and then record the outcome.)

_____

_____

_____

Have you had a session with yourself recently to check in and review your progress in working on worry management skills?

Yes _____   No _____

If not, can you schedule such a session with yourself?

Yes _____   No _____

List the date, time, and location: _____

_____

Preventing Lapses from Turning into Relapses

Sometimes, even with good planning, you may find that worry and anxiety have crept back into your life and started to become problematic again. Although this can be frustrating, it's important to remember that even if you're having a problematic lapse, this doesn't necessarily mean you're having a relapse. As mentioned earlier, the difference between a lapse and relapse is your reaction to renewed or heightened symptoms. So how you view the lapse, and yourself because of the lapse, will probably determine what you'll do next. Try not to be hard on yourself for experiencing a lapse. Perhaps you went through a difficult period in your life, got very busy and didn't have time to practice the skills you've learned, or simply forgot to practice them. Whatever the reason, you can turn the situation around by taking action once again. If you can see a dip in your progress as part of your overall journey toward mastering anxiety and worry, you're more likely to feel motivated to recoup your gains right away, rather than giving up.

Managing a Relapse

If you've had a relapse, your anxiety, your worry, and the safety behaviors you engaged in before starting this workbook have returned. You probably feel that you've undone the good work you devoted to tackling your anxiety and worry, and perhaps you believe there's no point in starting all over again. For many people, falling back into old and unwanted habits is not only discouraging, it can also feel like being back at square one. Fortunately, this is not the case. First and foremost, realize that you *can't* go back to square one. You aren't the same person you were before you began working through this book. You now understand what GAD is and how your thoughts and behaviors can inadvertently maintain excessive worry and anxiety, and you also know a number of strategies to help you manage your symptoms. In other words, you don't need to start all over again because you can't "unlearn" what you've already learned.

You might also be concerned that it will take a long time to get back to where you were. After all, if you worked on the different strategies and exercises for the recommended amount of time, it probably took a month or two before you started to notice real changes in your life. As a result, you may be thinking it will take just as long to regain the progress you made. This also isn't the case. Learning CBT skills is like learning to ride a bicycle: once you know how, you don't have to put the training wheels on again, no matter how long it's been since you last rode a bike. So once you return to practicing the strategies in this workbook, you can expect to quickly start seeing improvements in your ability to manage your worry and anxiety.

Developing a Coping Plan for Relapse

Managing a relapse isn't all that different from managing a lapse in symptoms. The hardest part is deciding to put forth the effort to recoup your hard-earned gains. Once you've made the decision to do so, it's a good idea to spend a week monitoring your worries and safety behaviors. This will allow you to get a good picture of your current functioning. You might actually find that you aren't worrying as much as you think you are, or that your lapse isn't as severe as you thought. Based on what your self-monitoring reveals, you can make a plan of action by assigning yourself exercises to begin working on. This might include general strategies, such as engaging in consistent self-care, or more specific exercises, such as problem solving, conducting behavioral experiments to challenge negative beliefs about uncertainty, or practicing written exposure.

Because relapses can feel discouraging, it's a good idea to dedicate consistent effort to overcoming them over the course of a few weeks, so as to build momentum. In practical terms, this means aiming to set a regular time each week to review your exercises and schedule new ones (a session with yourself, as described in exercise 11.2). Once you start feeling renewed confidence in your ability to master excessive worry, keep checking in with yourself every few weeks in order to ensure that you continue to maintain your gains.

EXERCISE 12.3: Plans for Overcoming a Relapse

Sometimes the hardest part of overcoming a relapse is not getting started, but sticking with the work once you start. Therefore, it's helpful to have some concrete and realistic steps to follow to get back on your chosen path and stay there. This exercise will help you create just such a plan for yourself. We recommend revisiting your plan and revising it as appropriate anytime you feel you're experiencing a relapse. (To download this worksheet for future use, visit http://www.newharbinger.com/31519.)

Step 1: Monitoring Worry and Safety Behaviors

Spend one week tracking your worries and safety behaviors. Try to record your findings three times a day in order to get a good picture of your symptoms. You can use the Safety Behaviors Monitoring Form from exercise 6.1 for this purpose (available for download at http://www.newharbinger.com/31519).

Step 2: Identifying Problem Areas

Write down any safety behaviors you identified as problematic, as well as any particular worries that strike you as excessive.

Problematic safety behaviors: _____

_____

_____

Excessive worries: _____

_____

_____

Step 3: Identifying Stressors and Neglected Self-Care

Because a relapse can be initially triggered by an increase in stress, it's a good idea to also record whether you've been experiencing any stressors, as well as whether you've been keeping up with good self-care. If you aren't sure whether you've been experiencing any significant stresses recently, you can refer to exercise 12.1 to help you identify any changes in your daily life that might lead to increased stress.

Recent stressors: _____

_____

_____

Self-care activities that you typically do but haven't done lately: _____

_____

_____

If you don't typically engage in self-care activities, review possibilities you listed in exercise 11.1, then record any activities that seem realistic for you to engage in:

_____

_____

_____

_____

Step 4: Scheduling a First Exercise

Based on your answers to the previous questions, you can now decide on a realistic first step toward recovering your earlier gains. What you do doesn't matter as much as beginning to move forward, so you can focus on addressing any of the problem areas you've identified. Here are some suggestions for your first exercise:

- **Scheduling self-care:** For example, you might go for a daily walk, always take the time to eat lunch, or get together with friends or family.

- **Addressing stressful situations:** For example, can you reduce your workload or delegate tasks to others?

- **Conducting behavioral experiments:** A good first step is to engage in behavioral experiments that you successfully accomplished in the past. This will allow you to gain momentum quickly and gives you a good opportunity to see yourself making up lost progress.

- **Addressing specific worries:** Depending on the worries you've recorded in recent monitoring, you might find that a good first step is to tackle specific worries through problem solving, written exposure, or challenging positive beliefs about the function of worry.

Record the first exercise you'll conduct over the next week:

_____

Step 5: Establishing a Consistent Time for a Session with Yourself

As a final step, set up a weekly time to review how your exercise worked out. Was it successful? If not, why not? During your session, assign yourself another exercise for the next week. If your first exercise was relatively easy to complete, you might want to choose two exercises for the coming week (for example, behavioral experiments and consistent self-care activities). However, don't overload yourself. It's better to go slow and successfully accomplish your goals than to try to do too many things at once and find that you're unable to follow through.

Date and time of check-in session:

_____

You can use the agenda suggested in exercise 11.2 when conducting your session with yourself (available for download at http://www.newharbinger.com/31519). Most importantly, be sure to consistently schedule new sessions with yourself for at least a few weeks to ensure that you're monitoring your progress and moving forward.

Learning from Your Mistakes

Although it's frustrating to experience dips in progress, both lapses and relapses can actually be helpful in the long run because they afford you the opportunity to identify what set you back in the first place. Armed with this knowledge, you'll be in a better position to avoid lapses in the future. So be sure to take some time to think about what was occurring in your life before you started to notice an increase in anxiety and worry. Perhaps you were dealing with problems at home or at work. Maybe a significant change in your schedule impacted your overall stress level, or maybe you'd stopped practicing some of the exercises that you'd been working on. The factors you identify as triggers for your lapse can then serve as early warning signs for future potential lapses, allowing you to target them right away. In the long run, recognizing bumps in the road early on can prevent you from running into them in the future and will ultimately increase your chances of building upon your gains over time.

One Final Note

We often tell our clients that they are a work in progress. Managing mental health is a lifelong process that you'll have to work on to a greater or lesser degree depending on the circumstances in your life. However, if you keep up with the strategies in this workbook, you'll probably see some significant changes in your life—not just in terms of less worry and anxiety, but also in terms of your general approach to daily life and its uncertainties.

One of the greatest benefits of cognitive behavioral therapy is that all the successes you have with it are entirely due to your own efforts. In this book, we've just provided the path; you're the one who chooses to walk it and keep moving forward. So take some time to reward yourself for all of your successes and gains. We recommend occasionally looking back at some of the earliest exercises you completed when you started this workbook and comparing them to those you're doing now. It's easy to lose perspective and forget how far you've come. Seeing that your early exercises would now be effortless, or at least relatively easy, can be very encouraging, and provides the motivation you may sometimes need to keep moving forward in the years ahead. Good luck!

Acknowledgments

First and foremost, I would like to thank my coauthor, Dr. Michel Dugas. Whenever I think about the work I've done in the field of GAD, I always think of the expression "standing on the shoulders of giants," and for me, one of those giants is Dr. Dugas. He is a brilliant researcher and clinician who has taught me more than I can say and has shaped me as a clinical psychologist. Michel, you have a thoughtful philosophy behind everything you do, be it mentoring graduate students, teaching classes, conducting research, or treating clients. To this day, all of my work is influenced by your approach to the many aspects of being a psychologist. I know that without your knowledge, support, and encouragement, I wouldn't have had the courage to share my ideas and ultimately complete this workbook. Thank you always.

The development of the strategies in this workbook would not have been possible without the excellent work conducted by many researchers (too many to mention) spanning over two decades at Université Laval, Concordia University, and most recently at the Université du Québec en Outaouais. For my part, I'd like to thank my former compatriots in the Anxiety Disorders Laboratory at Concordia University, including Kristin Buhr, Naomi Koerner, Kathryn Sexton, Kylie Francis, Nina Laugesen, and Mary Hedayati. I continue to remember fondly our daily lunchtime discussions. Much of the early research completed by our team in Michel's lab helped to shape the content of this book. Naomi, your excellent research on exposure in GAD was of great help in ensuring that the strategies presented in this book adhere to current empirical findings. Kristin, we have worked together for many years now, and I can't express how much I value your clinical knowledge and your friendship.

I'd like to thank some of my colleagues who, over the years, have helped me make sense of my ever-expanding conceptualization of GAD. My sincerest gratitude to Maureen Whittal and Jack Rachman, whom I first had the honor to work with at the former Anxiety Disorders Clinic at the University of British Columbia Hospital. I'm proud to continue to work with you today. Maureen and Jack, you not only taught be how to be a CBT therapist but were also kind enough to talk to me about my ideas and encourage me in my endeavors over the years. Thank you to Sarah Newth, David Jacobi, Adam Radomsky, Ram Randhawa, and Clare Philips; you have all been wonderful friends, and your clinical knowledge and insights have helped me better formulate my current clinical ideas. I consider myself lucky to know and have worked with such a wonderful group of people. Sarah, you were particularly helpful in thinking through an early conceptual model of GAD with me, which allowed me to develop the theory I work with today.

I'd also like to thank Dr. Peter McLean, who originally brought me to Vancouver and helped set me on my current career path. You were a wonderful clinician, and an inspiring, kind, and generous person with great vision. I am only one among many who continue to miss you and remember you with great affection.

Thank you to everyone at New Harbinger who helped us throughout the process of completing this workbook. In particular, I'd like to thank Jess O'Brien, who oversaw the progress of the work and ensured that I stayed on track and kept to my deadlines while also providing positive feedback every step of the way. Thanks also to Nicola Skidmore, Jess Beebe, and Marisa Solís for excellent editorial suggestions that allowed me to keep a clear focus when writing and to always keep the reader in mind. I'd also like to thank Matt McKay for offering us the opportunity to write this book in the first place.

Last but not least, I'd like to thank all of the people I have seen over the years who struggled with GAD, at Sacré-Coeur Hospital in Montreal, the Anxiety Disorders Clinic at UBC Hospital, and in private practice at the Vancouver CBT Centre. Thanks to you, I have learned a great deal about GAD and hopefully have become a better psychologist because of our work together. It is the work that I did collaboratively with my clients that assisted me in developing many of the treatment strategies that ultimately ended up in this workbook. I continue to be awed by the great courage present in those who choose to face their fears head-on and seek out a better life for themselves.

—Melisa Robichaud

I would first like to thank all of the clients and research participants I've come to know over the years. Your courage, resiliency, and willingness to take risks have impressed me and taught me more than you know. To all the people who participated in our treatment studies, thank you so much for putting up with our obsessive attention to detail, and for helping us develop helpful treatment options for other people who suffer from GAD.

I would also like to acknowledge my doctoral students over the years: Naomi Koerner, Kristin Anderson, Kristin Buhr, Sonya Deschênes, Eleanor Donegan, Kylie Francis, Elizabeth Hebert, Nina Laugesen, Kathryn Sexton, and, of course, Melisa Robichaud. It has been such a pleasure to work with each one of you on your piece of the "anxiety puzzle." I would like to thank those of you who continue to collaborate (and put up) with me—most notably, Melisa. Thank you so much for inviting me to take this journey with you. It has been a pleasure and an honor to work with you on this wonderful project.

A heartfelt thank-you to all the colleagues who have collaborated with me over the years. During my time at Concordia University (1998 to 2013), I was lucky enough to collaborate with William Bukowski, Jean-Philippe Gouin, Natalie Phillips, Andrew Ryder, and my good friend Adam Radomsky. You have all helped me expand my horizons and think about how our different areas of interest are, in fact, not that different. I must also thank my colleagues at Sacré-Coeur Hospital, where most of our clinical trials were conducted. Special thanks to Isabelle Geninet, Amélie Seidah, Pascale Harvey, and Renée Leblanc; you are truly wonderful therapists. I would also like to thank my new colleagues at the Université du Québec en Outaouais. Thank you for your warm welcome and I look forward to many years of fruitful and exciting collaborations.

On a more personal note, I would like to thank my parents, Denise and Ronald, and my three sisters, Suzanne, Céline, and Joanne, for giving me the kind of developmental history that makes my life so much easier today. Thanks to you, I have never forgotten that science and compassion for human suffering can go hand in hand.

Finally, I would like to thank my wife, Céline, and my two children, Sophie and Jérémie. This book is dedicated to you because you are simply my raison d'être.

—Michel J. Dugas

References

American Psychiatric Association. 2013. *Diagnostic and Statistical Manual of Mental Disorders*, 5th ed. Washington, DC: American Psychiatric Association.

Birrell, J., K. Meares, A. Wilkinson, and M. Freeston. 2011. "Toward a Definition of Intolerance of Uncertainty: A Review of Factor Analytical Studies of the Intolerance of Uncertainty Scale." *Clinical Psychology Review*, 31: 1198–1208. DOI:10.1016/j.cpr.2011.07.009.

Dugas, M. J., M. H. Freeston, M. D. Provencher, S. Lachance, R. Ladouceur, and P. Gosselin. 2001. "Le questionnaire sur l'inquiétude et l'anxiété: Validation dans des échantillons non cliniques et cliniques" [The Worry and Anxiety Questionnaire: Validation in Non-clinical and Clinical Samples]. *Journal de Thérapie Comportementale et Cognitive*, 11: 31–36.

Dugas, M. J., F. Gagnon, R. Ladouceur, and M. H. Freeston. 1998. "Generalized Anxiety Disorder: A Preliminary Test of a Conceptual Model." *Behaviour Research and Therapy*, 36: 215–226. doi: 10.1016/S0005-7967(97)00070-3.

Dugas, M. J., and M. Robichaud. 2007. *Cognitive-Behavioral Treatment for Generalized Anxiety Disorder: From Science to Practice*. New York: Routledge.

Dugas, M. J., P. Savard, J. Turcotte, A. Gaudet, P. Brillon, R. Ladouceur, R. Leblanc, and N. J. Gervais. 2010. "A Randomized Clinical Trial of Cognitive Behavioral Therapy and Applied Relaxation for Adults with Generalized Anxiety Disorder." *Behavior Therapy*, 41: 46–58. doi: 10.1016/j.beth.2008.12.004.

D'Zurilla, T. J., and A. M. Nezu. 2007. *Problem-Solving Therapy: A Positive Approach to Clinical Intervention*. New York: Springer.

Goldman, N., M. J. Dugas, K. A. Sexton, and N. J. Gervais. 2007. "The Impact of Written Exposure on Worry: A Preliminary Investigation." *Behavior Modification*, 31: 512–538. doi: 10.1177/0145445506298651.

Gosselin, P., R. Ladouceur, C. M. Morin, M. J. Dugas, and L. Baillargeon. 2006. "Benzodiazepine Discontinuation Among Adults with GAD: A Randomized Trial of Cognitive-Behavioral Therapy." *Journal of Consulting and Clinical Psychology*, 74: 908–919. doi: 10.1037/0022-006X.74.5.908.

Inglis, I. R. 2000. "The Central Role of Uncertainty Reduction in Determining Behaviour." *Behaviour*, 137: 1567–1599.

Koerner, N., and M. J. Dugas. 2006. "A Cognitive-Affective Model of Generalized Anxiety Disorder: The Role of Intolerance of Uncertainty." In G. C. L. Davey and A. Wells (eds.), *Worry and Psychological Disorders: Theory, Assessment, and Treatment* (pp. 201–216). Chichester, UK: John Wiley and Sons.

Ladouceur, R., M. J. Dugas, M. H. Freeston, E. Léger, F. Gagnon, and N. Thibodeau. 2000. "Efficacy of a Cognitive-Behavioral Treatment for Generalized Anxiety Disorder: Evaluation in a Controlled Clinical Trial." *Journal of Consulting and Clinical Psychology*, 68: 957–964. doi: 10.1037/0022-006X.68.6.957.

Ladouceur, R., M. J. Dugas, M. H. Freeston, J. Rhéaume, F. Blais, F. Gagnon, N. Thibodeau, and J. M. Boisvert. 1999. "Specificity of Generalized Anxiety Disorder Symptoms and Processes." *Behavior Therapy*, 30: 191–207. doi: 10.1016/S0005-7894(99)80003-3.

Lavy, E., and M. van den Hout. 1990. "Thought Suppression Induces Intrusions." *Behavioural Psychotherapy*, 18: 251–258.

Lee, A. Y. 2001. "The Mere Exposure Effect: An Uncertainty Reduction Explanation Revisited." *Personality and Social Psychology Bulletin*, 10: 1255–1266.

Nezu, A. M., C. M. Nezu, and T. J. D'Zurilla. 2007. *Solving Life's Problems: A Five-Step Guide to Enhanced Well-Being*. New York: Springer.

Robichaud, M., and M. J. Dugas. 2005. "Negative Problem Orientation (Part I): Psychometric properties of a new measure." *Behaviour Research and Therapy*, 43: 391–401. doi: 10.1016/j.brat.2004.02.007.

Salkovskis, P., D. Clark, and M. Gelder. 1996. "Cognition-Behaviour Links in the Persistence of Panic." *Behaviour Research and Therapy*, 34: 453–458.

Sexton, K. A., and M. J. Dugas. 2009. "Defining Distinct Negative Beliefs About Uncertainty: Validating the Factor Structure of the Intolerance of Uncertainty Scale." *Psychological Assessment*, 21: 176–186. doi: 10.1037/a0015827.

Wegner, D. M. 1994. "Ironic Processes of Mental Control." *Psychological Review*, 101: 34–52.

Wenzlaff, R. M., and D. M. Wegner. 2000. "Thought Suppression." *Annual Review of Psychology*, 51: 59–91. doi: 10.1146/annurev.psych.51.1.59.

Melisa Robichaud, PhD, is a clinical psychologist and cofounder of the Vancouver CBT Centre. She holds adjunct clinical faculty and clinical associate positions in psychology and psychiatry at the University of British Columbia and Simon Fraser University. Robichaud specializes in the treatment of anxiety with an emphasis on generalized anxiety disorder (GAD), and is on the scientific advisory board of AnxietyBC. For over a decade, she has provided workshops and training to both mental health professionals and the public on the treatment of GAD, and has published numerous book chapters and scientific articles on the subject.

Michel J. Dugas, PhD, is professor of psychology at the Université du Québec en Outaouais, and affiliate professor of psychology at Concordia University. Over the past two decades, he has conducted research on the etiology and treatment of generalized anxiety disorder (GAD) with a specific focus on intolerance of uncertainty. He has published over ninety scientific articles and made more than 250 conference presentations on the topic of GAD. Dugas is a Fellow of the Canadian Psychological Association and the Canadian Association of Cognitive and Behavioural Therapies.

Foreword writer **Martin M. Antony, PhD**, is professor and chair in the department of psychology at Ryerson University in Toronto, Ontario. He is director of research at the Anxiety Treatment and Research Clinic at St. Joseph's Healthcare in Hamilton, Ontario, and past president of the Canadian Psychological Association. An awardwinning researcher, Antony is coauthor of *The Shyness and Social Anxiety Workbook*, *When Perfect Isn't Good Enough*, and more than twentyfive other books. His research, writing, and clinical practice focus on cognitive behavioral therapy (CBT) and the treatment of anxiety disorders. He has been widely quoted in the American and Canadian media.

FROM OUR PUBLISHER—

As the publisher at New Harbinger and a clinical psychologist since 1978, I know that emotional problems are best helped with evidence-based therapies. These are the treatments derived from scientific research (randomized controlled trials) that show what works. Whether these treatments are delivered by trained clinicians or found in a self-help book, they are designed to provide you with proven strategies to overcome your problem.

Therapies that aren't evidence-based—whether offered by clinicians or in books—are much less likely to help. In fact, therapies that aren't guided by science may not help you at all. That's why this New Harbinger book is based on scientific evidence that the treatment can relieve emotional pain.

This is important: if this book isn't enough, and you need the help of a skilled therapist, use the following resources to find a clinician trained in the evidence-based protocols appropriate for your problem. And if you need more support—a community that understands what you're going through and can show you ways to cope—resources for that are provided below, as well.

Real help is available for the problems you have been struggling with. The skills you can learn from evidence-based therapies will change your life.

Matthew McKay, PhD
Publisher, New Harbinger Publications

**If you need a therapist, the following organization
can help you find a therapist trained in cognitive behavioral therapy (CBT).**

The Association for Behavioral & Cognitive Therapies (ABCT) Find-a-Therapist service offers a list of therapists schooled in CBT techniques. Therapists listed are licensed professionals who have met the membership requirements of ABCT and who have chosen to appear in the directory.

Please visit www.abct.org and click on *Find a Therapist*.

**For additional support for patients, family, and friends,
please contact the following:**

Anxiety and Depression Association of American (ADAA)
please visit www.adaa.org

National Alliance on Mental Illness (NAMI)
please visit www.nami.org

Register your **new harbinger** titles for additional benefits!

When you register your **new harbinger** title—purchased in any format, from any source—you get access to benefits like the following:

- Downloadable accessories like printable worksheets and extra content

- Instructional videos and audio files

- Information about updates, corrections, and new editions

Not every title has accessories, but we're adding new material all the time.

Access free accessories in 3 easy steps:

1. Sign in at NewHarbinger.com (or **register** to create an account).

2. Click on **register a book**. Search for your title and click the **register** button when it appears.

3. Click on the **book cover or title** to go to its details page. Click on **accessories** to view and access files.

That's all there is to it!

If you need help, visit:

NewHarbinger.com/accessories

new harbinger
CELEBRATING
40 YEARS